To Mary & Chris
With my love
and thanks —

Cherrie
October — 1981.

ALLEN LANE/GODFREY CAVE ASSOCIATES

A VICTORIAN FLOWER ALBUM

GOD'S FLORAL GEMS, GLISTENING
ON THE VERDANT FACE OF NATURE.

COLLECTED AND PAINTED IN THE
SUMMER EVENINGS OF 1873,
AS A PLEASING RECREATION.

BY

HENRY TERRY.

At the end of the book appears a complete and correct list of
the flowers and insects illustrated, compiled by Richard Pankhurst and
Paul Whalley of the British Museum (Natural History).

ALLEN LANE
Penguin Books Ltd
17 Grosvenor Gardens
London SW1W 0BD
in association with
Godfrey Cave Associates Ltd.
42 Bloomsbury Street
London WC1

First published in 1978

Copyright © Godfrey Cave Associates Ltd, 1978
Foreword © Bridget Boland, 1978

ISBN *0 7139 1145 x*

Printed in Great Britain by
W. S. Cowell Ltd.
Ipswich, Suffolk

BEAUTIFUL children of the woods and fields!
That bloom by mountain streamlets 'neath the heather
Or into clusters 'neath the hazels gather—
Or where by hoary rocks you make your bields,
And sweetly flourish on through summer weather—
          I love you all!

Beautiful flowers! to me ye fresher seem
From the Almighty hand that fashion'd all,
Than those that flourish by a garden—wall;
And I can image you, as in a dream,
Fair, modest maidens, nursed in hamlets small—
          I love you all!

Beautiful things ye are, where'er ye grow!
The wild red-rose—the speedwell's peeping eyes—
"My own blue-bell"—the daisy, that doth rise
Wherever sunbeams fall or winds do blow;
And thousands more, of blessed   forms and dyes—
          I love you all!

Beautiful nurslings of the early dew,
Fann'd in your loveliness by every breeze,
And shaded o'er by green and arching trees;
I often wish'd that I were one of you,
Dwelling afar upon the grassy leas—
          I love ye all!

x x x x x x x x x x x x x x x x x x x x x x x x x

Ye o'er my heart have thrown a lovesome spell;
And though the worldling, scorning, may deride
          I love ye all!

ROBERT NICOLL.

The parts that constitute a flowering plant.

ROOT, Fibrous, bulbous, tuberous &c, ringed, tufted or fibrous, tuberous, bulbous, spindle &c

STEM, simple & compound, underground, horizontal, compound, simple, ascending, creeping

LEAF, lancet, oval, sessile, arrow-head, palmate, linear, conate

decurrent, pinnate, radiate, paltate, perfoliate, serrate

crenate, partite, ternate, toothed, fringed,

CALYX, or flower-cup, wallflower, loosestrife, labiate, poppy

COROLLA, or FLOWER, salver shaped, funnel, wheel, bell, trumpet

labiate, compound, cruciform

STAMENS, stamens have two parts, filament & anther, 1 filament, 2 anther

PISTIL, comprise the ovary, style, & sti 2 1 style, 2 stigma, 3 ovary.

RECEPTACLE,

NECTARY, That portion of a flower where the honey is secreted — spurs of a Columbine &c

STIPULE, BRACTS x bracts, x spurs

To.

Emily, Annie, and Harry.

My dear children, to you I dedicate these rude Transcripts of Nature, though fully conscious of their demerits I know you will appreciate my efforts, for you know the difficulties and labour with which I have had to contend in collecting and painting them. I am pleased that you inherit my enthusiastic love of Nature and the Beautiful. You have joined me in my Wild-Flower Excursions over the beautiful uplands and luxurious lowlands that surround this grand old city — you have watched my labours with loving interest and cheering word, to you therefore I present the result, feeling that when myself, like Wild-Flowers, have passed from off the face of God's lovely earth, you will open these leaves with interest and affection for your Father.

Oxford Octr. 1873.

FOREWORD
by
Bridget Boland

Here, gentle reader, is a book to make gentle readers of us all. This dear book, originally called *Wild Flowers from the Neighbourhood of Oxford*, was made with love by a father for his children, painting wildflowers they found in English meadows and commons near their home, and it brings fresh air and sunshine into any room with it, dispelling any mood but its own with sure enchantment. Just as surely, the author lives and breathes for us. True to his period, he has a Victorian improving intent of course, revealed at the beginning by his page dissecting botanically the parts of flowers, but then that page never was quite finished. Did the children at his elbow clamour too eagerly to have their finds painted at once? Could he himself not wait to enjoy the delight of the delicate, exquisitely accurate recording, while meaning always to go back and ink that first page over? His children live too, the pretty, solemn little objects representing 'Spring' and 'Summer'. Look at the loving skill with which the hawthorn blossom is painted (p. 21), and the steady hand that records the 'exotic' that has seeded itself on the Bishop of Oxford's lawn (p. 100); and then look at the daffodil (p. 27) and the poppy and meconopsis (p. 84): it is not possible that these are by the same hand, and surely Papa failed to resist the pleas of Anne and Emily to let them paint 'the easy bits' of those larger flowers? There is no portrait of Harry in the book, but perhaps he would not sit so still as those good little girls would do; and suddenly, for a few pages only, we have paintings of insects, butterflies, moths, a caterpillar whose movement is beautifully observed: perhaps these record a brief collector's passion in Harry.

I feel that Papa often went flower-hunting with the children, for I doubt if he would have turned them loose alone on the Bishop's lawn; and when Histon bog proved unproductive of wildflowers in April and again in May it was surely he who showed the children the ugly but interesting mushroom and the sphagnum moss. The Latin names are there, of course, for educational purposes, but in these days of superbly illustrated botanical encyclopedias we may forget what a hunt through many herbals Mr Terry must have had to identify some of the less common of these flowers. I see him, his big book under his arm, trudging to the Bodleian Library, or perhaps to some expert at the Oxford Botanical Gardens for help.

Though his paper is of the excellent handmade quality that best reflects the light through transparent watercolours, it is not of a pure white that would have enabled him to use it, left uncovered, for his highlights; so he used Chinese white for these, laying it on in an extraordinarily thick impasto for such white florets as those of the hawthorn and the meadowsweet. He never mixed it, though, with colours, which (except in the chrome, the only opaque colour he used) explains the wonderful luminosity of the paintings. His colours were also all permanent – no carmines, fugitive greens, or modern anilines of course, in his paintbox! Wildflowers do often seem brighter than those we see in gardens, perhaps because we come upon them with surprise, but can even the real borage someone's fingers found in the grass more than a hundred years ago have been a more wonderful blue than that in its portrait here? We are lucky that the book was a family treasure for the descendants of his elder daughter, not left in some dank attic where the paper would have become badly foxed; and it was because it had been loved and used that the cover had become much worn, and one of the family took it to a bookshop to ask advice on getting it rebound, where the publisher happened to see it and pounced on it.

Unhappily, very little is known with any certainty about Henry Terry himself. While not a parson, he is thought by his family to have had some connection with ecclesiastical buildings, not as an architect, possibly as a diocesan surveyor. He was twice married, and in later life lived in various places in Norfolk. There is a Henry Terry who exhibited watercolours at the Academy and other London galleries between 1870 and 1885 whose identity for a moment raised hopes; but all his catalogued works are portraits, which were not our Henry's forté, and Harry would have been too young for the earlier entries. But if this book is his only memorial, the creator of it was surely a man who would have been happy to know he would lead us too, with his children, through those Oxfordshire fields.

1

SPRING

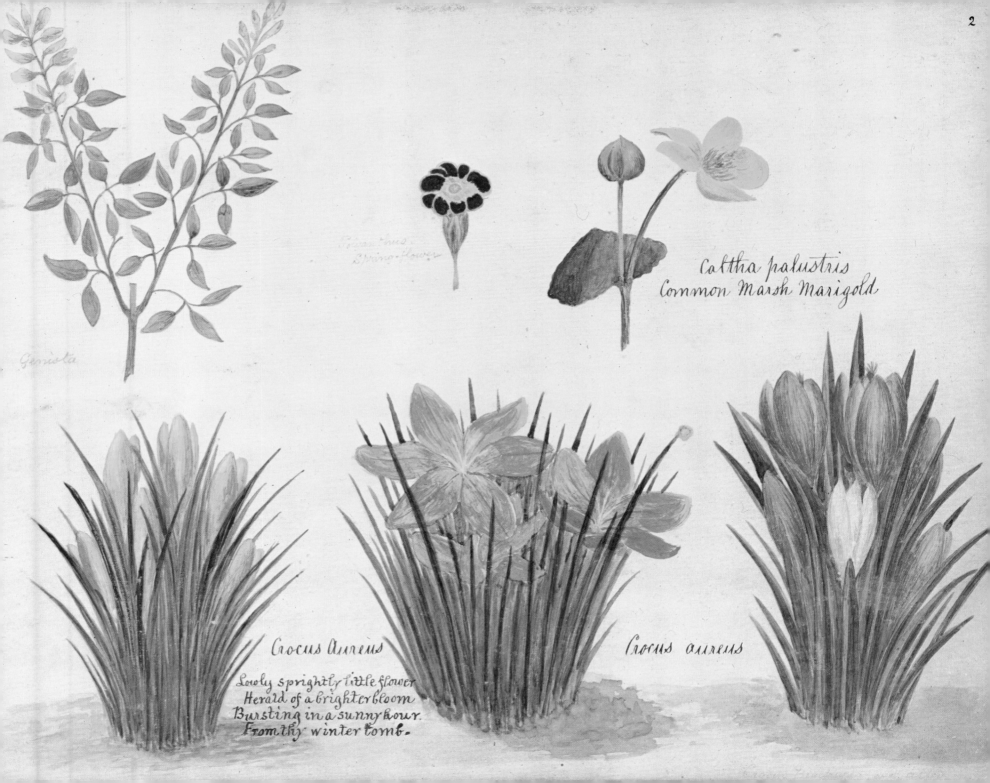

Genista

Primulus
Spring-flower

Caltha palustris
Common Marsh Marigold

Crocus Aureus

Lovely sprightly little flower
Herald of a brighter bloom
Bursting in a sunny hour,
From thy winter tomb.

Crocus aureus

3

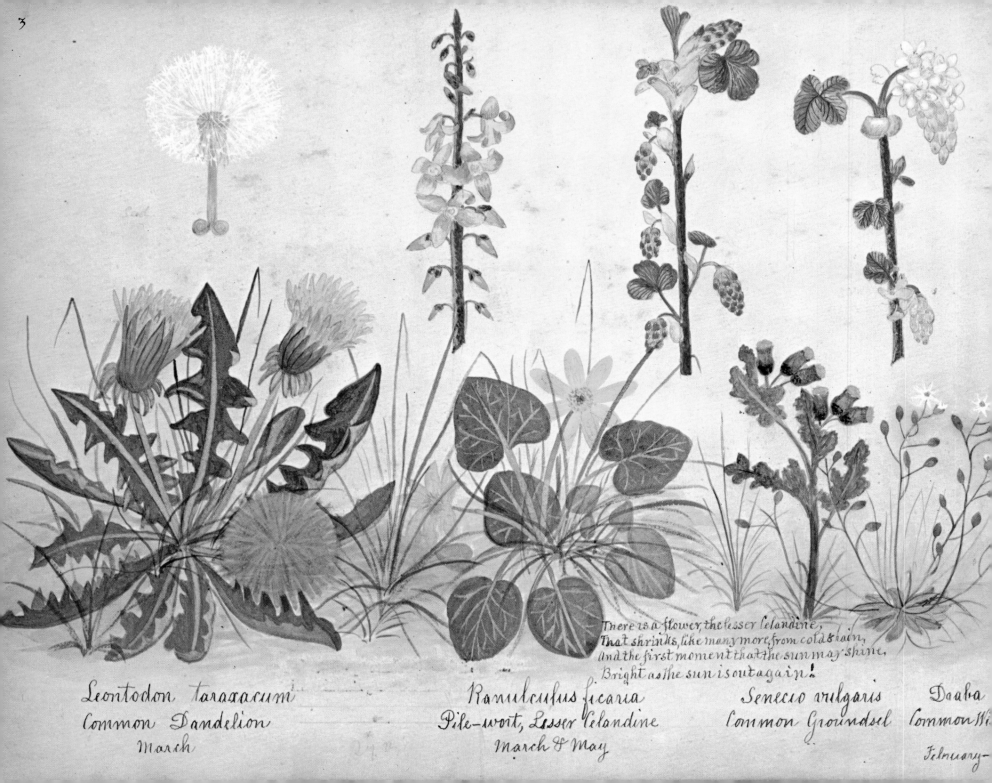

There is a flower, the lesser celandine,
That shrinks, like many more, from cold & rain,
And the first moment that the sun may shine,
Bright as the sun is out again!

Leontodon taraxacum
Common Dandelion
March

Ranunculus ficaria
Pile-wort, Lesser Celandine
March & May

Senecio vulgaris
Common Groundsel

Draba
Common W
February

Lemium maculatum
Spotted Dead-nettle

Eranthis hyemalis
Winter Aconite
March
Perennial

Jalanthus nivalis
Snowdrop
January — March
Perennial

Tussilago Farfara
Colts-foot
March — April
Perennial

Anemone nemorosa
Wood Anemone
March — May
Perennial

5

Ranculus japonica

Capsella Bursa Pastoris
Common Shepherds Purse
Flowers nearly all the year round
Annual

Mercurialis perennis
Dog's Mercury
April — May
Perennial

Nepeta Glechoma
Ground Ivy
April — June
Perennial

Fragaria vesca
Wood Strawberry
May — July
Perennial

Adoxa Moschatellina
Common Moschatell
April — May
Perennial

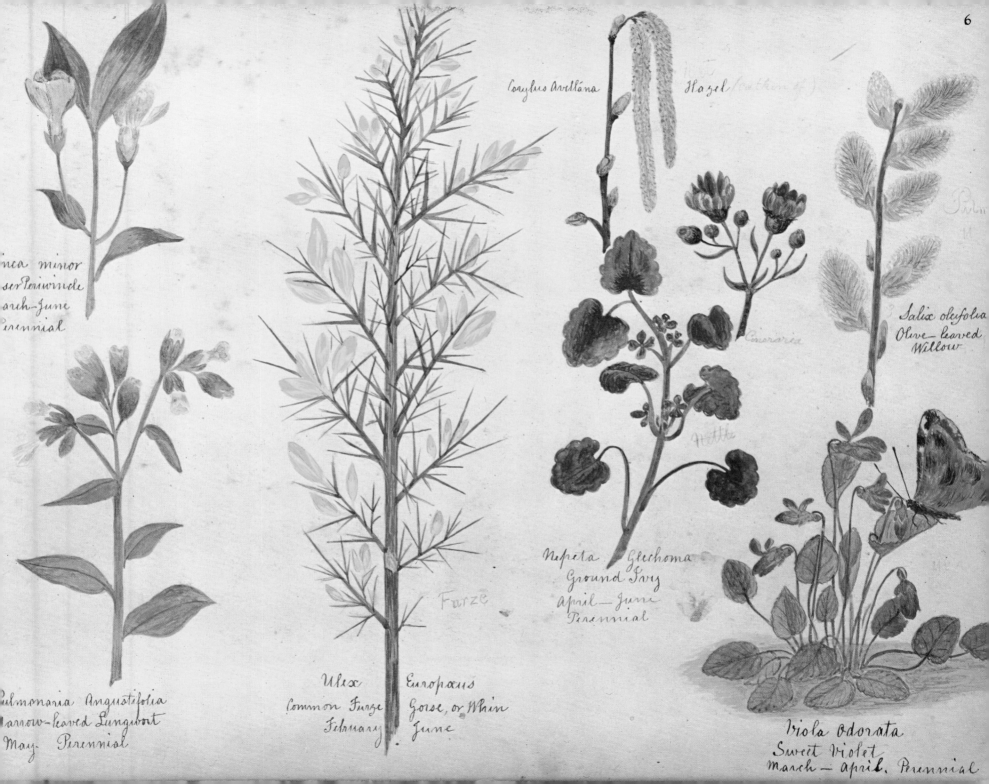

Corylus Avellana   Hazel (catkin of)

...nca minor
...ser Periwinkle
...arch—June
...Perennial

Salix oleifolia
Olive—leaved
Willow

Cineraria

Nepeta   Glechoma
Ground Ivy
April — June
Perennial

Pulmonaria Angustifolia
Narrow—leaved Lungwort
May. Perennial

Ulex   Europæus
Common Furze   Gorse, or Whin
February   June

Furze

Viola Odorata
Sweet Violet
March — april. Perennial

Galium Aparine
Goose Grass Cleavers
June — August
Annual.

Plantago media
Hoary Plantain
June — July
Perennial.

Primula vulgaris
Common Primrose
March — May
Perennial.

Cardamine Pratensis
Cuckoo flower or Ladie's Smock
May.   Perennial
~~Meadowsweet~~

Primula Veris
April—May

Cowslip, Paigle
Perennial

Bellis Perennis, Common Daisy
Flowers nearly all the year round

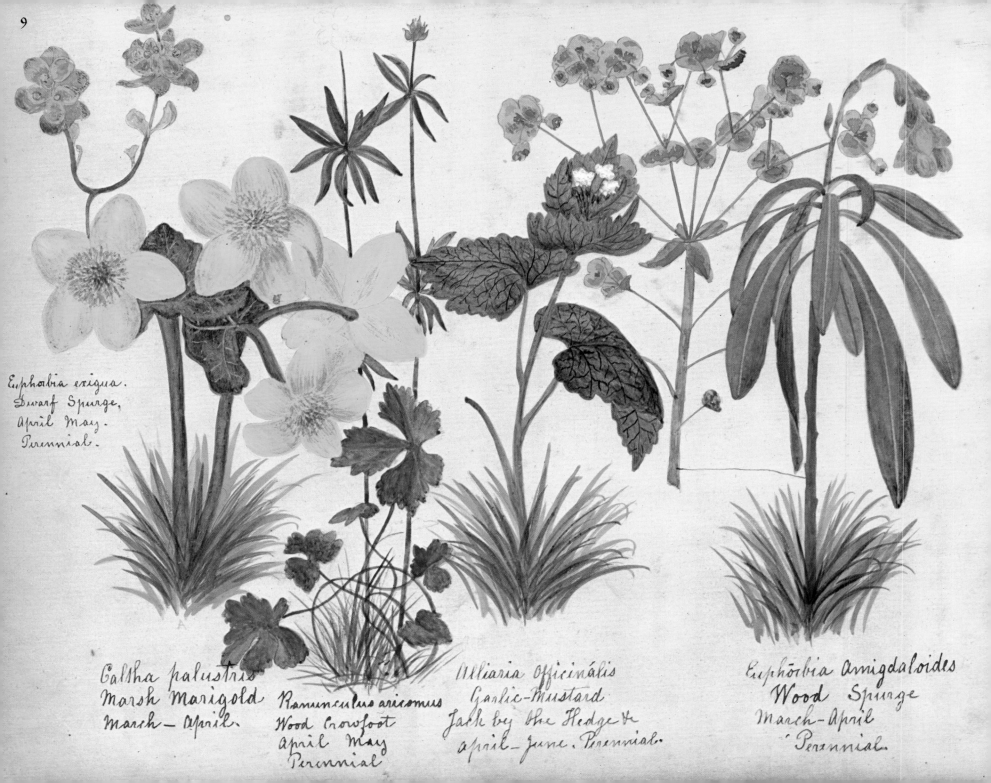

Euphorbia exigua.
Dwarf Spurge,
April May.
Perennial.

Caltha palustris
Marsh Marigold
March – April.

Ranunculus auricomus
Wood Crowfoot
April May
Perennial

Alliaria officinalis
Garlic-Mustard
Jack by the Hedge &
April – June. Perennial.

Euphorbia Amigdaloides
Wood Spurge
March – April
Perennial.

Fritillaria Meleagris, Fritillary, or Snake's-head. A rare plant but common in the meadows between Oxford & Iffley, also in the Isle of White. April. Perennial. Root, bulbous scaly.

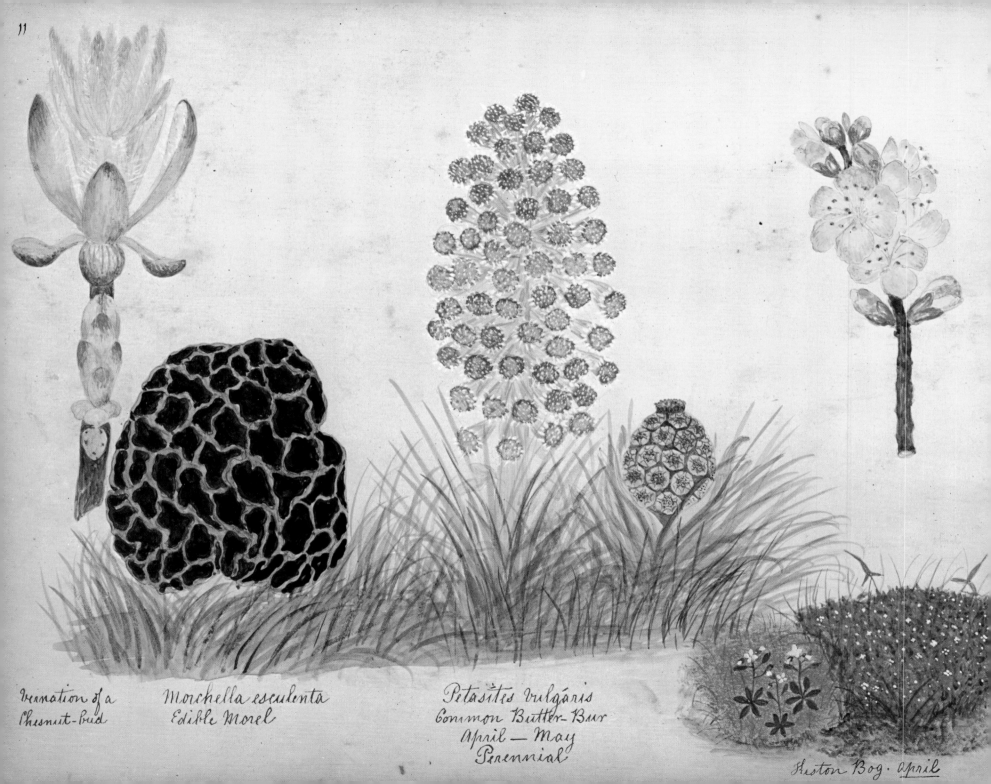

11

Vernation of a
Chesnut-Bud

Morchella esculenta
Edible Morel

Petasites vulgaris
Common Butter-Bur
April — May
Perennial

Keston Bog. April

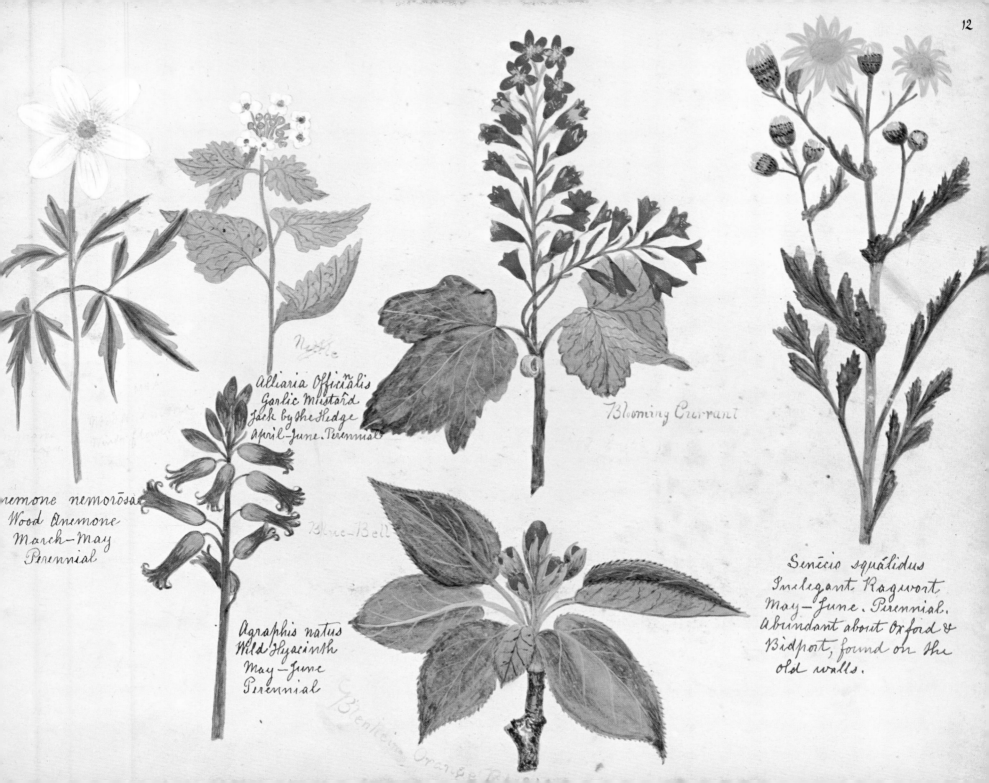

Nettle

Alliaria Officinalis
Garlic Mustard
Jack by the Hedge
April–June. Perennial

Blooming Currant

nemone nemorosa
Wood Anemone
March–May
Perennial

Blue–Bell

Agraphis natus
Wild Hyacinth
May–June
Perennial

Blenheim Orange

Senecio squalidus
Inelegant Ragwort
May–June. Perennial.
Abundant about Oxford &
Bidport, found on the
old walls.

13

Nepeta Glechoma.
Ground Ivy.
April — June,
Perennial.

Lamium purpureum.
Purple Dead Nettle.
Flowers all the summer.
Perennial.

Veronica hederifolia.
Ivy-leaved Speedwell.
Flowers all the summer.
Perennial.

Stellaria Holostea.
Greater Stitchwort, Satin-flower or
adder's-meat. May — June.
Perennial.

Milk-maid (real)

Geranium molle.
Dove's-foot Crane's-bill.
Flowers all the summer.
Annual.

Sherardia arvensis
Field Madder
June–August
Annual

Plantago lanceolata
Ribwort Plantain
June – July
Perennial

Erodium cicutarium.
Hemlock Stork's-bill.
Flowers all the Summer.
Annual.

Brassica Rapa
Common Turnip

Ranunculus acris.
Meadow Crowfoot.
June – July.
Perennial.

Stellaria media.
Chickweed.
Flowers all the year round.
Annual.

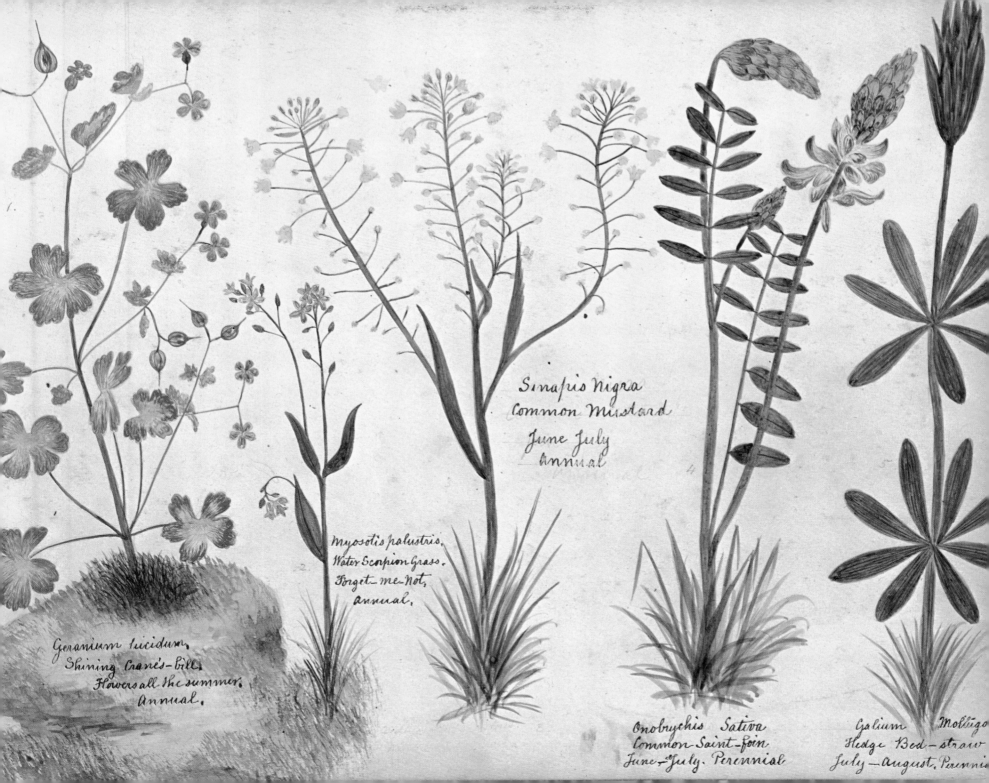

Sinapis Nigra
Common Mustard
June July
Annual

Myosotis palustris.
Water Scorpion Grass.
Forget-me-Not,
Annual.

Geranium lucidum.
Shining Crane's-bill.
Flowers all the summer.
Annual.

Onobrychis Sativa
Common Saint-foin
June & July. Perennial

Galium
Hedge Bed-straw
July—August, Perennial

Mollugo

Capsella Bursa Pastoris.
Common Shepherds Purse.
Flowers nearly all the year round.
Annual.

Lamium amplexicaule.
Henbit Dead-nettle.
Flowers all the summer.
Perennial.

Viola canina.
Dog violet.
April — July.
Perennial.

Pyrus Malus.
Crab-tree or Wild Apple.
May.
Tree.

Lychnis diurna.
Red Robbin, or Campion.
Flowers all the Summer.
Perennial.

Galeobdolon luteum.
Weasel-snout, Archangel, yellow dead-nettle.
May — July
Perennial.

Borago officinalis.
Common Borage.
June — September.
Biennial.

Silene inflata
Bladder Campion
June — August
Perennial.

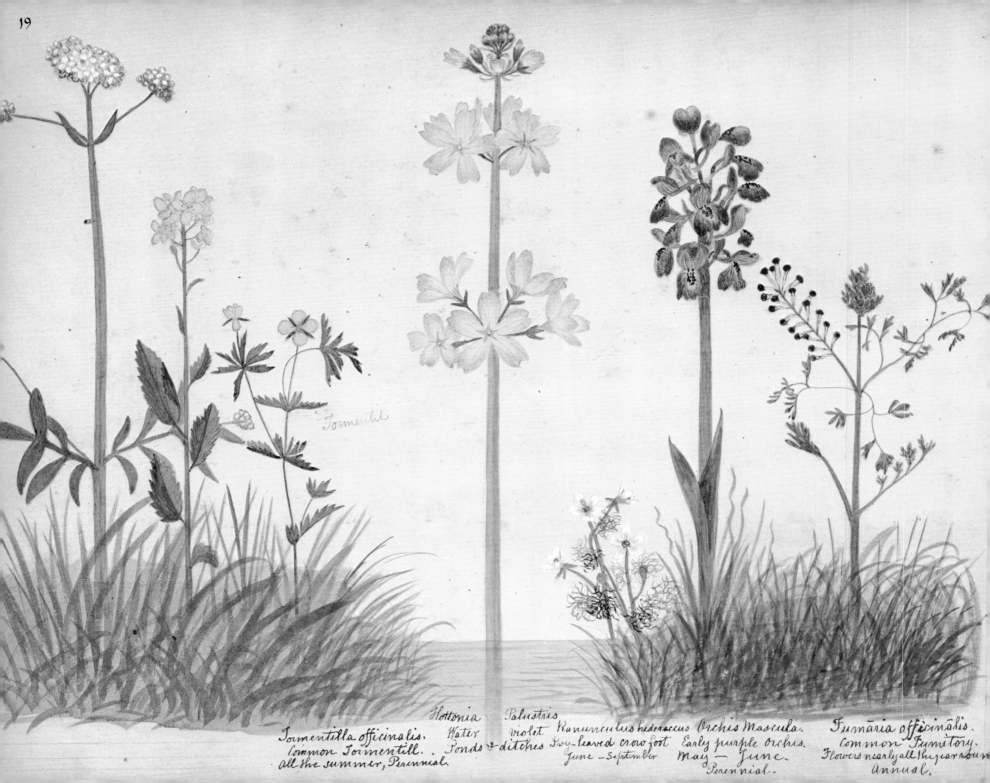

Tormentil

Hottonia Palustris
Water violet
Ponds & ditches

Tormentilla officinalis.
Common Tormentill.
All the summer, Perennial.

Ranunculus hederaceus
Ivy-leaved crow foot
June — September

Orchis Mascula.
Early purple Orchis.
May — June.
Perennial.

Fumaria officinalis.
Common Fumitory.
Flowers nearly all the year round
Annual.

Cerostium umbellatum
(Ragged Chichweed) ?

Linaria Cymbalaria.
Ivy–leaved Toad–flax,
Mother of thousands.
all the year round.
Perennial.

Draba verna.
Vernal Whitlow–grass.
February — May.
Annual.

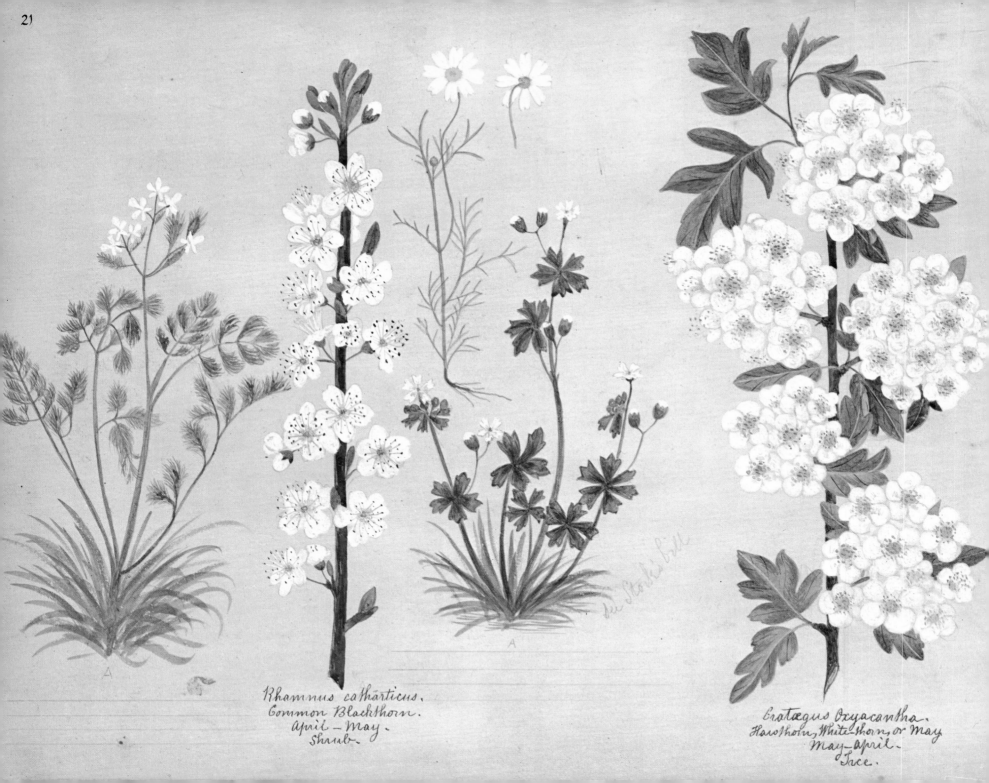

Rhamnus catharticus.
Common Blackthorn.
April — May.
Shrub.

Cratægus Oxyacantha.
Hawthorn, White-thorn, or May.
May — April.
Tree.

Vicia Cracca.
Tufted Vetch.
July – August.
Perennial.

Bryonia dioica.
White Bryony.
May – August.
Perennial.

23

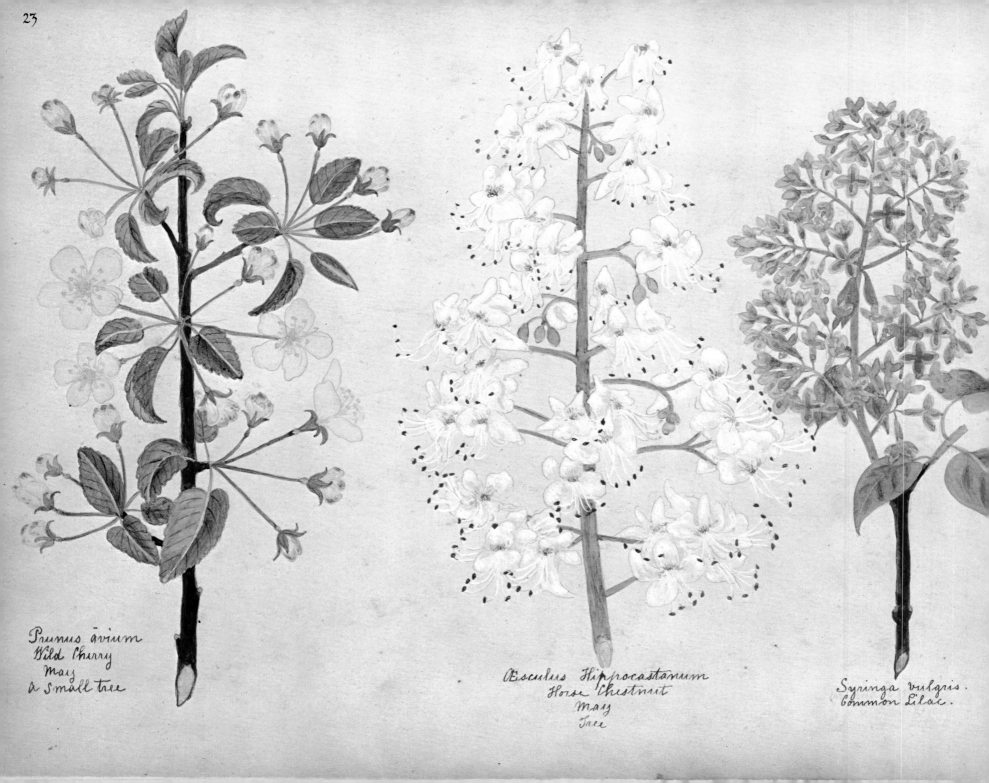

Prunus avium
Wild Cherry
May
a Small tree

Æsculus Hippocastanum
Horse Chestnut
May
Tree

Syringa vulgris.
Common Lilac.

Campion

Pinguicula vulgaris.
Common Butterwort.
June, Perennial.

Scorpion grass

spheards Purse   Trifolium medium.   Trifolium filiforme.   Lychnis diurna.
                        Zigzag Clover   Lesser Yellow Trefoil. Red Robin, or Campion.   Field Sorrel
                                                                    All the summer. Perennial.

Equisetum fluviatile
Great Water Horse Tail.

Myosotis Arvensis.
Field Scorpion grass.
June — August.
Annual.

Arum maculatum.
Cuckoo-pint, Wake-Robin
Lords and Ladies.
May — June, Perennial.

Chelidonium majus.
Common Celandine.
All the summer.
Perennial.

Barbarea vulgaris.
Common Winter Cress.
May — August.
Perennial.

Serrátula tinctória.
Common Saw-wort.
August.
Perennial.

Galium verum.
Yellow Bed-straw.
July — August.
Perennial.

Centauréa cyanus
Corn Blue-Bottle or Corn-flower
July-August — October November
Annual or Biennial

Fumaria officinális.
Common Fumitory.
Flowers nearly all the year round.
Annual.

27

Narcissus, Pseudo Narcissus.
Common Daffodil.
March – April.
Perennial.

Daffodil.

Potentilla Anserina.
Silver-weed, Goose-grass.
June – July.
Perennial.

Pedicularis sylvatica.
Dwarf Red-Rattle, Marsh Lousewort.
June – August.
Perennial.

Tormentilla officinalis.
Common Tormentil.
Flowers all the summer.
Perennial.

Chrysanthemum Leucanthemum.
White Ox-eye.
June — July.
Perennial.

Asperula Odorata.
Sweet Woodruff.
May — June.
Perennial.

Symphytum officinale.
Common Comfrey.
May — August.
Perennial.

Laburnum

Chilidonium majus.
Common Celandine.
All the year round.
Perennial.

Ranunculus arvensis.
Corn Crowfoot.
June.
annual.

Ranunculus Bulbos
Bulbous Butterc...
May – June.
Perennial.

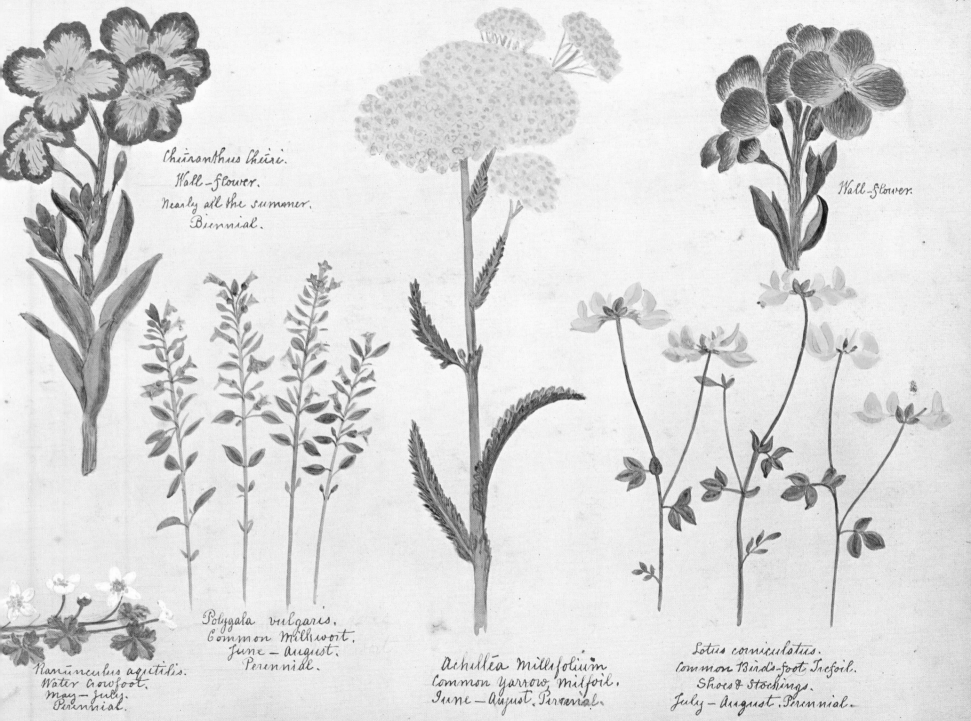

Cheiranthus Cheiri.
Wall-flower.
Nearly all the summer.
Biennial.

Wall-flower.

Ranunculus aquetilis.
Water Crowfoot.
May — July.
Perennial.

Polygala vulgaris.
Common Milkwort.
June — August.
Perennial.

Achillea Millefolium
Common Yarrow, Milfoil.
June — August. Perennial.

Lotus corniculatus.
Common Bird's-foot Trefoil.
Shoes & Stockings.
July — August. Perennial.

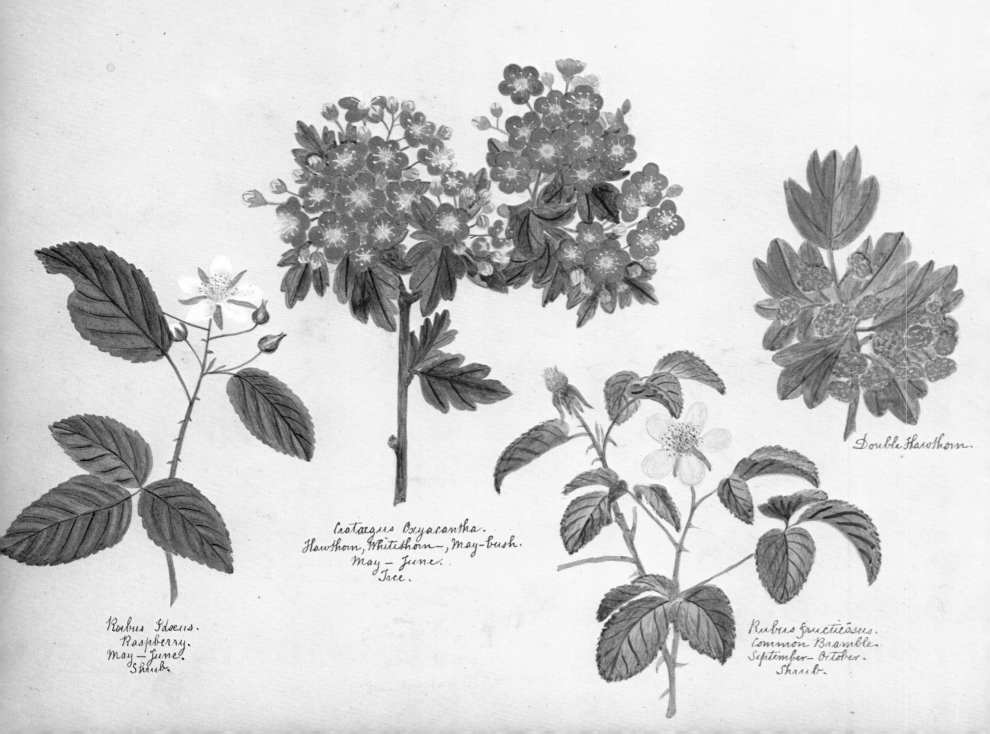

Crataegus Oxyacantha.
Hawthorn, Whitethorn—, May-bush.
May—June.
Tree.

Double Hawthorn.

Rubus Idaeus.
Raspberry.
May—June.
Shrub.

Rubus fructicosus.
Common Bramble.
September—October.
Shrub.

Rhinanthus crista-galli.
Cock's-comb, Yellow-rattle.
Haymaking begins when in full flower.
Annual.

Fragaria vesca.
Wood Strawberry.
May—June—July.
Perennial.

Orchis Pyramidalis.
Pyramidal Orchis.
July.
Perennial.

Vicia sepium.
Bush Vetch.
May—June.
Perennial.

Lotus Major.
Bird's foot Trefoil.
July—August.
Perennial.

Lysimachia nemorum.
Wood Loosestrife, Yellow Pimpernel.
June – July. Perennial.

Sherardia arvensis.
Field Madder.
June – August.
Annual

Veronica Beccabunga.
Brooklime
June – August.
Perennial.

arel

Stitchwort

Madder

Birds-c)

Viola tricolor
Pansy or Heartsease
Flowers all the summer, Annual.

Geranium Molle
Dove's-foot Cranes-bill
All the summer. Annual

Saxifraga umbrosa
London Pride
S. Patrick's Cabbage
Perennial

Erodium cicutarium.
Hemlock Storks-bill.
All the Summer. Annual.

Veronica Chamædrys.
Germander Speedwell.
Blue Speedwell, Bird's eye.
May, June. Perennial.

Pinguicula vulgaris.
Common Butter-wort.
June. Perennial.
The Bog, Headington.

Nasturtium officinale.
Common Water-cress.
June – August.
Perennial.

Ranunculus aquatilis.
Water Crowfoot.
May – July.
Perennial.

Polygala vulgaris.
Common Milkwort.
June – July.
Perennial.

Knautia arvensis
Field Scabious
July, August
Perennial.

Malva Sylvestris.
Common Mallow.
June - August.
Perennial

Convolvulus arvensis.
Field Bindweed.
June - July.
Perennial.

Prunella vulgaris.
Self - heal.
July — August.
Perennial.

Chrysanthemum segetum
Yellow Ox-eye, Corn Marigold
June-July-October
Annual.

Æsculus Hippocastanum.
Horse Chestnut.
May.
Tree.

Saxifraga granulata
White Meadow Saxifrage
Roots granulated
May June Perennial
Shotover Hill & St Marys Cray

inaria vulgáris.
ellow Toad-flax.
gust September.
Perennial.
ild Snap-dragon

Clematis Vitalba
Travellers Joy, Virgin-bower
May - June. Perennial.

Trifolium filiforme.
Lesser Yellow Trefoil.
June — July.
Annual.

common Saint-Foin &

Trifolium repens.
Dutch white Clover.
Through the summer.
Perennial.

Trifolium pratense
Purple Clover.
All the summer.
Perennial.

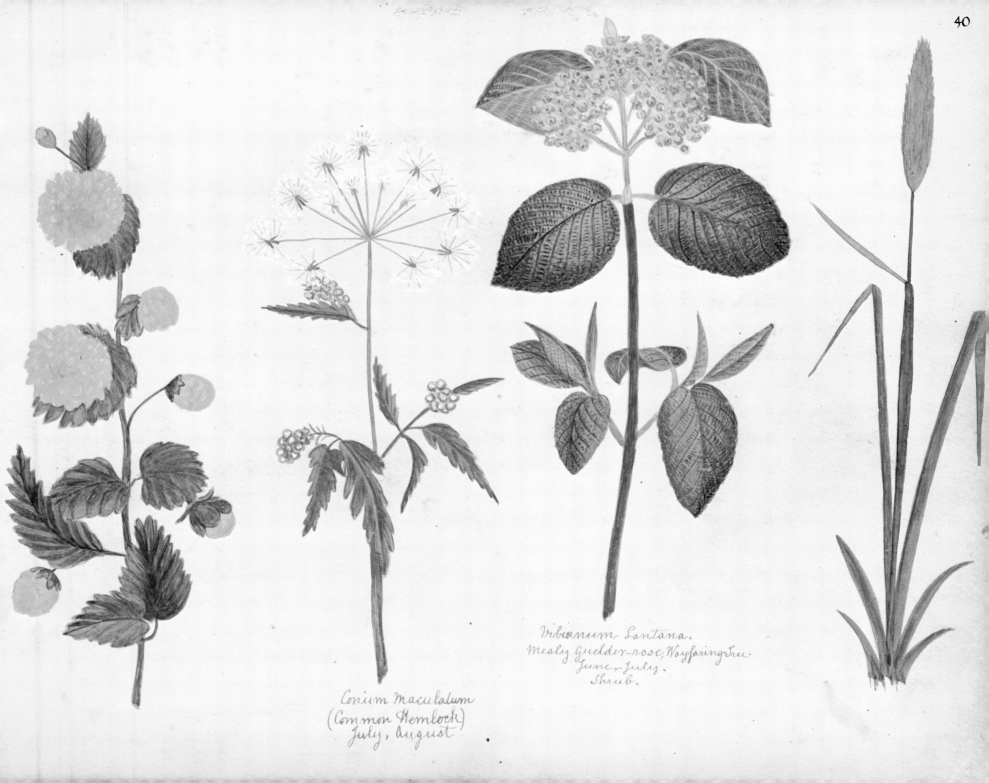

Conium maculatum
(Common Hemlock)
July, August

Viburnum Lantana.
Mealy Guelder-rose, Wayfaring Tree.
June–July.
Shrub.

41

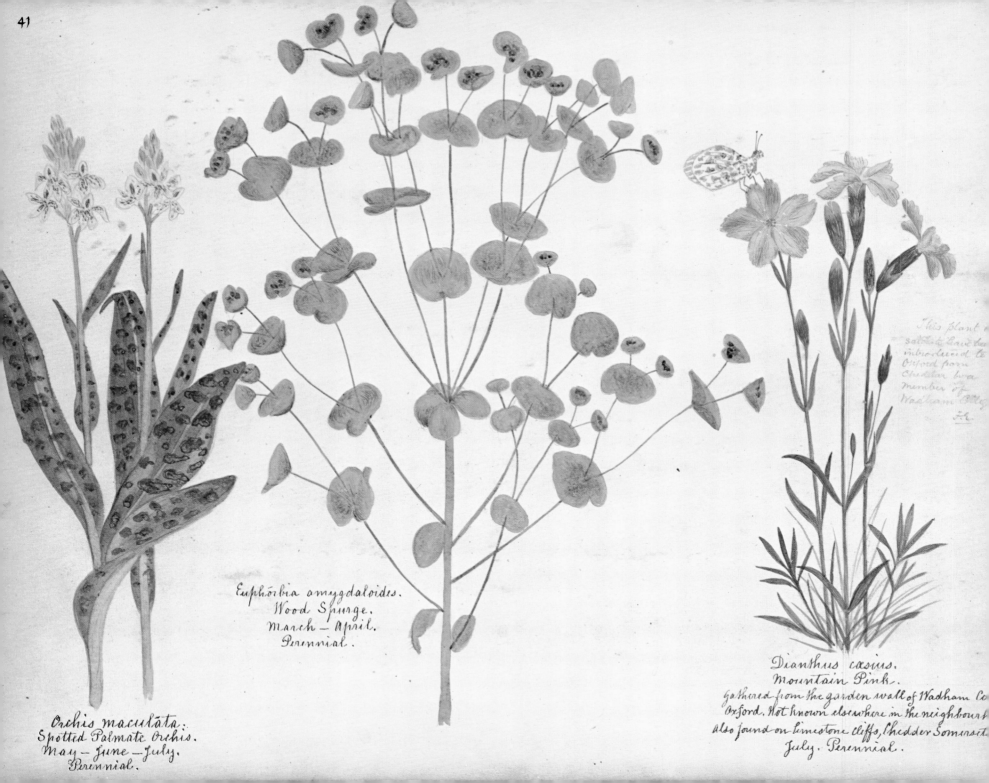

Euphorbia amygdaloides.
Wood Spurge.
March — April.
Perennial.

Orchis maculata.
Spotted Palmate Orchis.
May — June — July.
Perennial.

This plant
said to have been
introduced to
Oxford from
Cheddar by a
member of
Wadham Colleg
F.R.

Dianthus cæsius.
Mountain Pink.
Gathered from the garden wall of Wadham Co
Oxford. Not known elsewhere in the neighbourh
also found on limestone cliffs, Cheddar Somerset
July. Perennial.

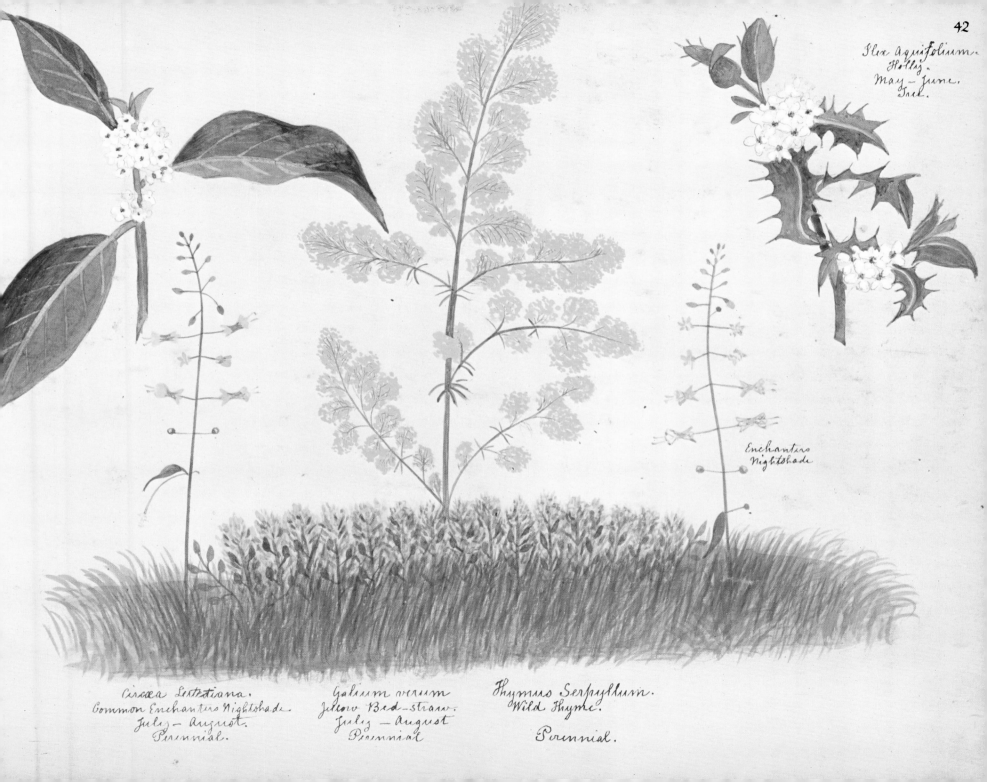

Ilex aquifolium.
Holly.
May – June.
Tree.

Enchanters
Nightshade

Circæa Lutetiana.
Common Enchanters Nightshade.
July – August.
Perennial.

Galium verum
Yellow Bed-straw.
July – August
Perennial

Thymus Serpyllum.
Wild Thyme.

Perennial.

yellow Vetch
Lathyrus pratensis
Meadow Vetchling
July, August
Perennial

Poterium Sanguisorba. Stellaria graminea.
Salad Burnet. Lesser Stitchwort.
July — August June — July.
Perennial. Perennial.

Exotic

Iris versicolor humesina.

Solanum Dulcamara.
Woody Nightshade, Bittersweet.
June — July.
Perennial.

Pinguicula vulgaris
Common Butterwort.
June — July. Perennial.

Briza.

Sweet Pea

Pea

Iris Pseud-ácorus.
Flower-de-Luce.
Yellow Iris, Corn Flag
June – July.
Perennial.

Pea

Campanula rotundifolia.
Hair-Bell.
July.—September.
Perennial.

Euphrasia Centaurium.
Common Centaury.
July.—August.
Annual.

Campanula Trachelium.
Nettle-leaved Bell-Flower, Canterbury Bells.
July.—August, September.
Perennial.

47

Orchis latifolia
Marsh Orchis
June–July
Wet places
Perennial.

Echium vulgāre
Common Viper's Bugloss
June–July.
Biennial
From a wood near
Stow-Wood
Oxon

Broom

Dyer's greenweed
July

From a ...

Sarothamnus scoparius.
Common Broom.
June.
Shrub.

Anthyllis Vulneraria.
Common Lady's Fingers.
June—August.
Perennial.

Narrow-leaved
Vitch

Listera ovata.
Twäblade.
June — August.
Perennial.
Headington Bog

Vicia sepium.
Bush Vitch.
May — June.
Perennial.

Geranium Robertianum.
Herb Robert.
flowers all the summer.
Annual.

Grass

grass

Ophrys apifera.
Bee Orchis.
June – July
Perennial.

51

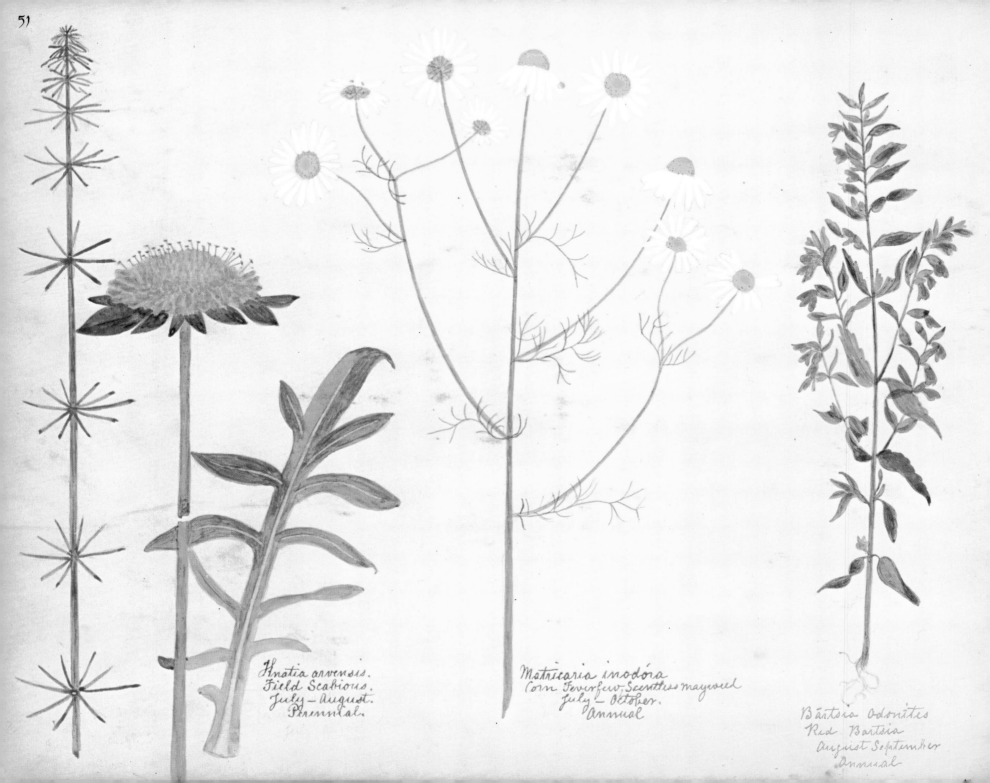

Knatia arvensis.
Field Scabious.
July — August.
Perennial.

Matricaria inodora
Corn Feverfew. Scentless mayweed
July — October.
Annual

Bartsia Odonites
Red Bartsia
August September
Annual

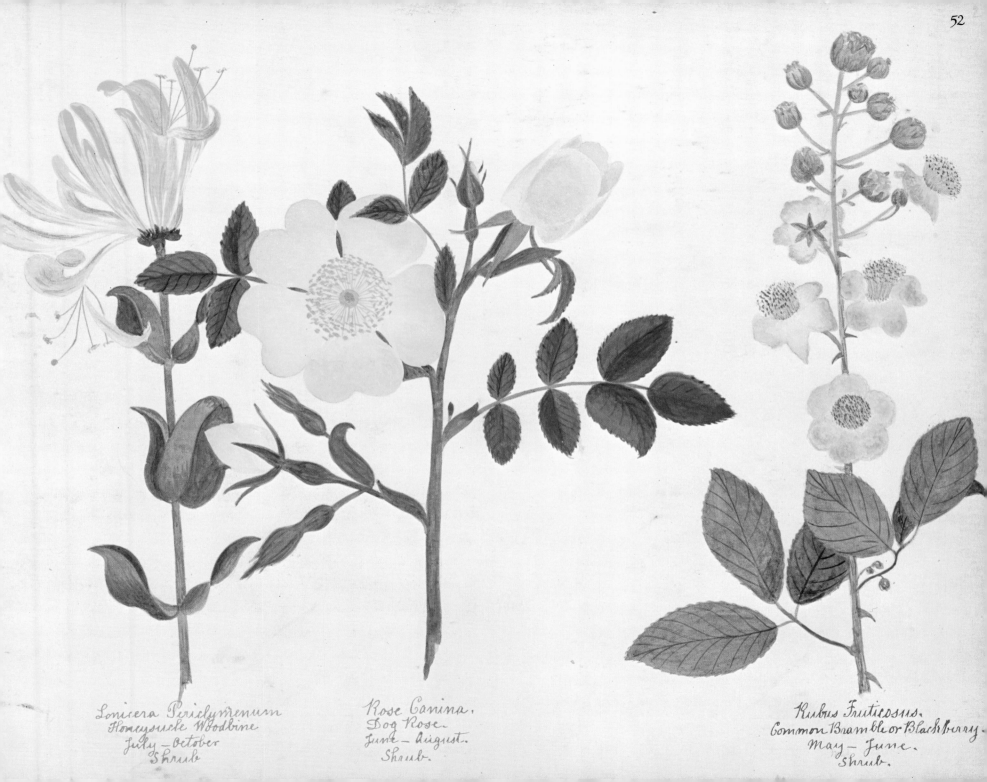

Lonicera Periclymenum
Honeysuckle Woodbine
July – October
Shrub

Rose Canina.
Dog Rose.
June – August.
Shrub.

Rubus Fruticosus.
Common Bramble or Blackberry.
May – June.
Shrub.

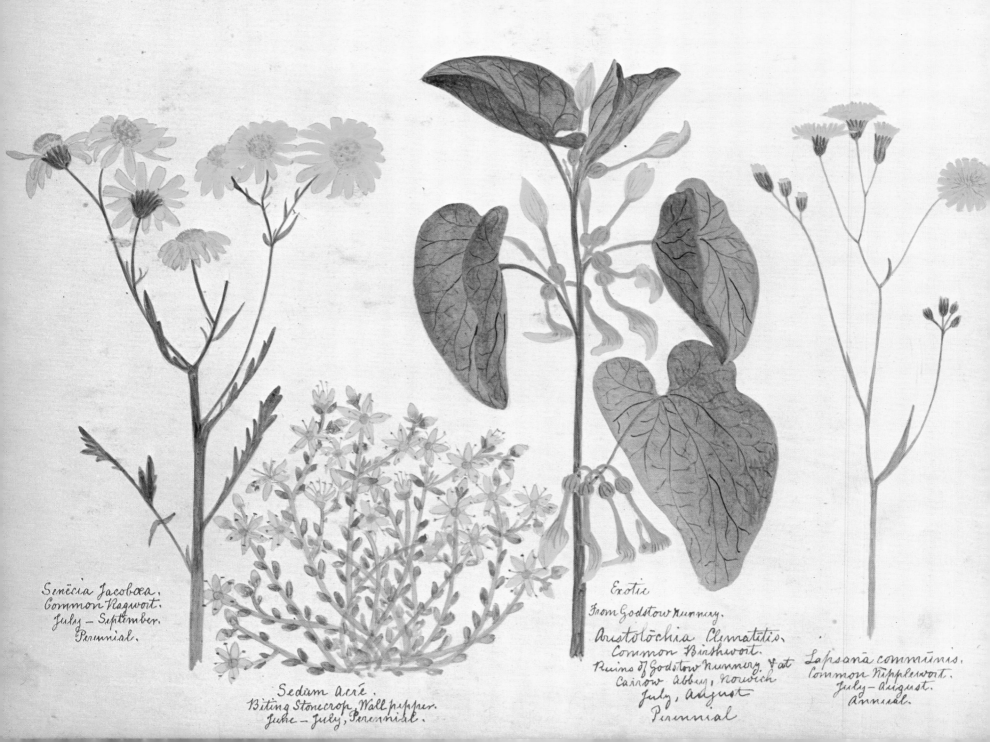

Senecia Jacobœa.
Common Ragwort.
July – September.
Perennial.

Sedum Acré.
Biting Stonecrop, Wall pepper.
June – July, Perennial.

Exotic
From Godstow Nunnery.
Aristolochia Clematitis.
Common Birthwort.
Ruins of Godstow Nunnery & at
Carrow Abbey, Norwich
July, August
Perennial

Lapsana communis.
Common Nipplewort.
July – August.
Annual.

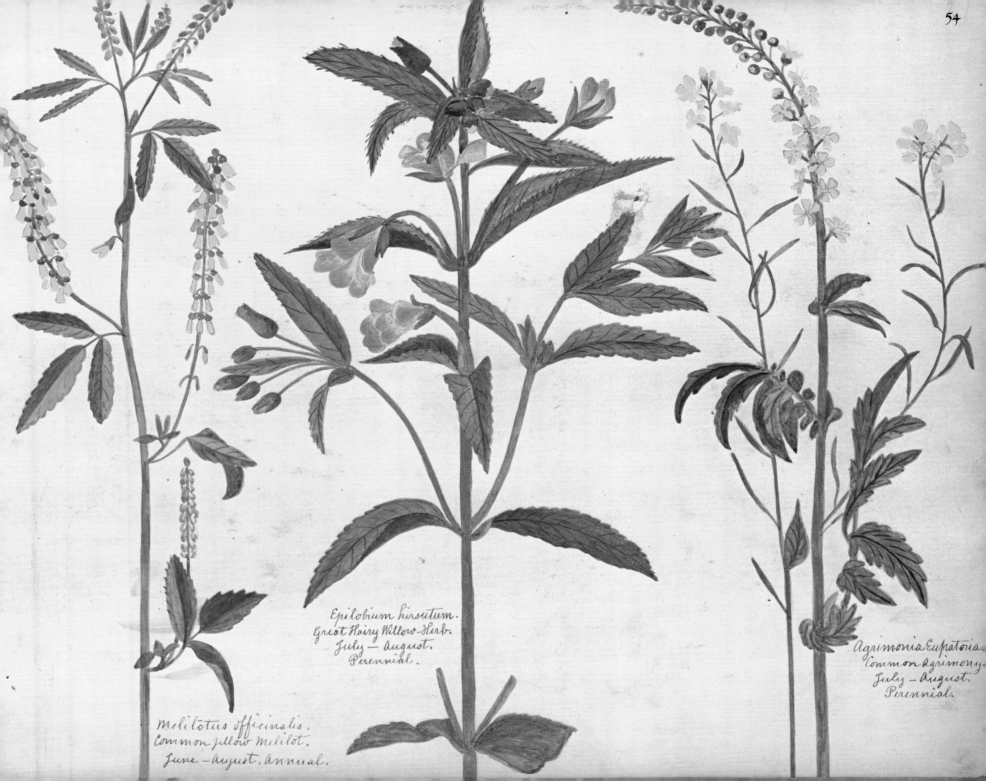

Epilobium hirsutum.
Great Hairy Willow-Herb.
July — August.
Perennial.

Agrimonia Eupatoria.
Common Agrimony.
July — August.
Perennial.

Melilotus officinalis.
Common yellow Melilot.
June — August. Annual.

55

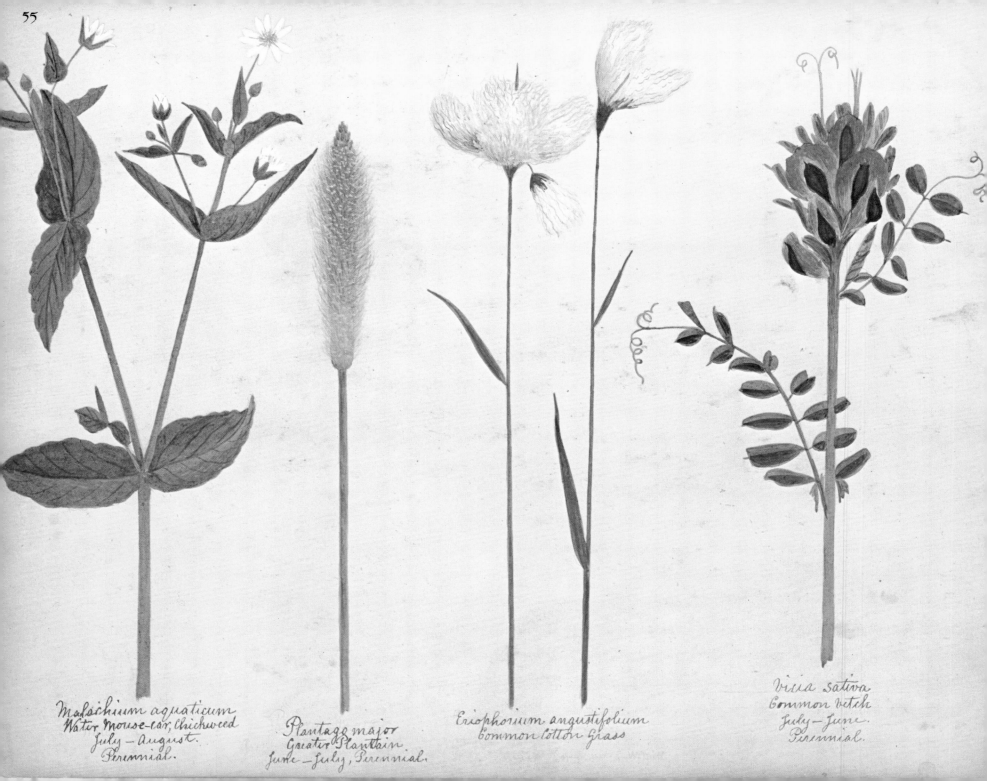

Malachium aquaticum
Water Mouse-ear, Chickweed
July — August.
Perennial.

Plantago major
Greater Plantain
June — July, Perennial.

Eriophorum angustifolium
Common Cotton Grass

Vicia sativa
Common Vetch
July — June.
Perennial.

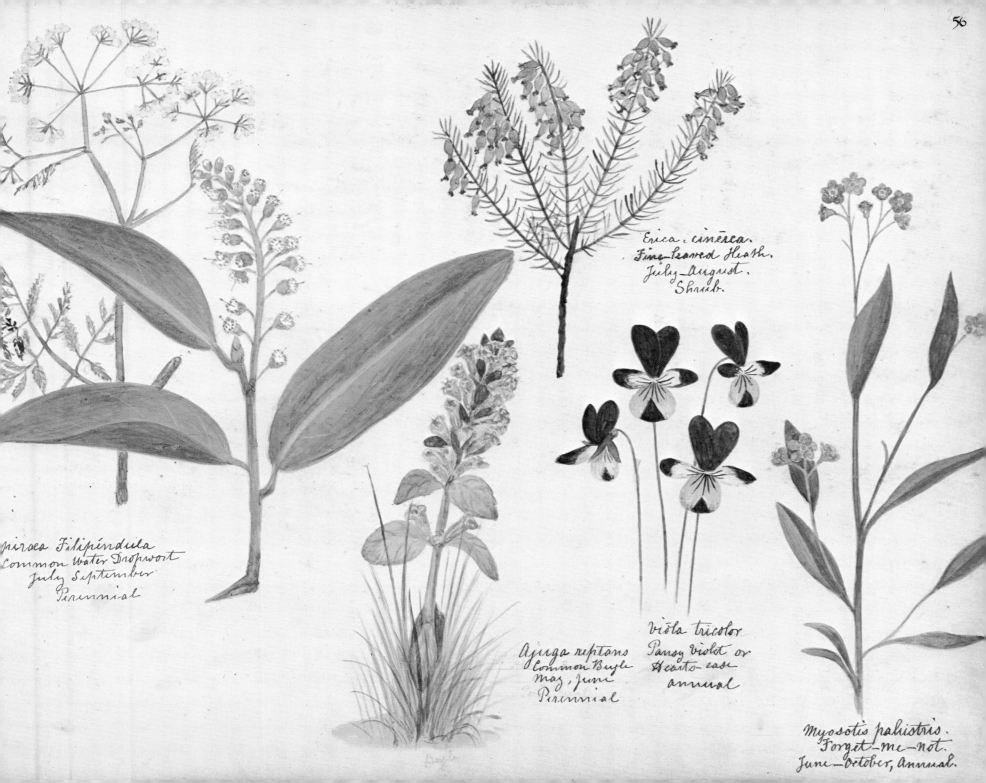

Erica cinerea.
Fine-leaved Heath.
July—August.
Shrub.

Spiræa Filipendula
Common Water Dropwort
July September
Perennial

Ajuga reptans
Common Bugle
May, June
Perennial

Viola tricolor
Pansy Violet or
Hearts-ease
annual

Myosotis palustris.
Forget-me-not.
June—October, Annual.

Bugle

57

Scutellaria galericulata.
Blue Scull-Cap.
July-September.
Perennial.

Geranium pratense
meadow crane's-bill
July August
Perennial.

Spiraea Filipendula
Dropwort
July September
Perennial

Melilotus officinalis.
Common yellow Melilot.
June-August-
Annual.

Calystegia sepium.
Great Bindweed.
July — September.
Perennial.

Butomus umbellatus.
Flowering Rush.
June — July.
Perennial.

Chrysanthemum
segetum
Corn Marigold
(Annual). ?

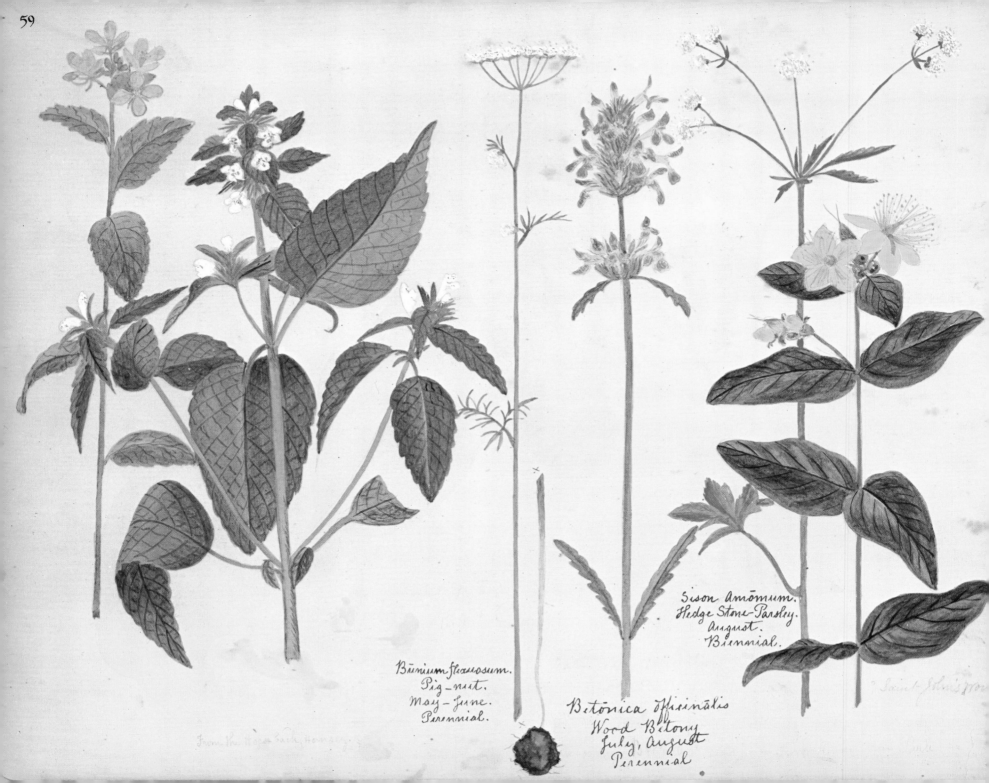

Būnium flexuosum.
Pig-nut.
May-June.
Perennial.

Sison Amōmum.
Hedge Stone-Parsley.
August.
Biennial.

Betónica officinālis
Wood Betony
July, August
Perennial

From the Rope Bank Horsey.

Saint John's Wort

Ranunculus bulbosus
Bulbous Crowfoot
Buttercup
Perennial

Aquilegia vulgaris.
Common Columbine.
June — July
Perennial.

Lychnis Flos-Cuculi.
Ragged Robin.
All the summer.
Perennial.

Juncus effusus
Soft Rush
July
Perennial

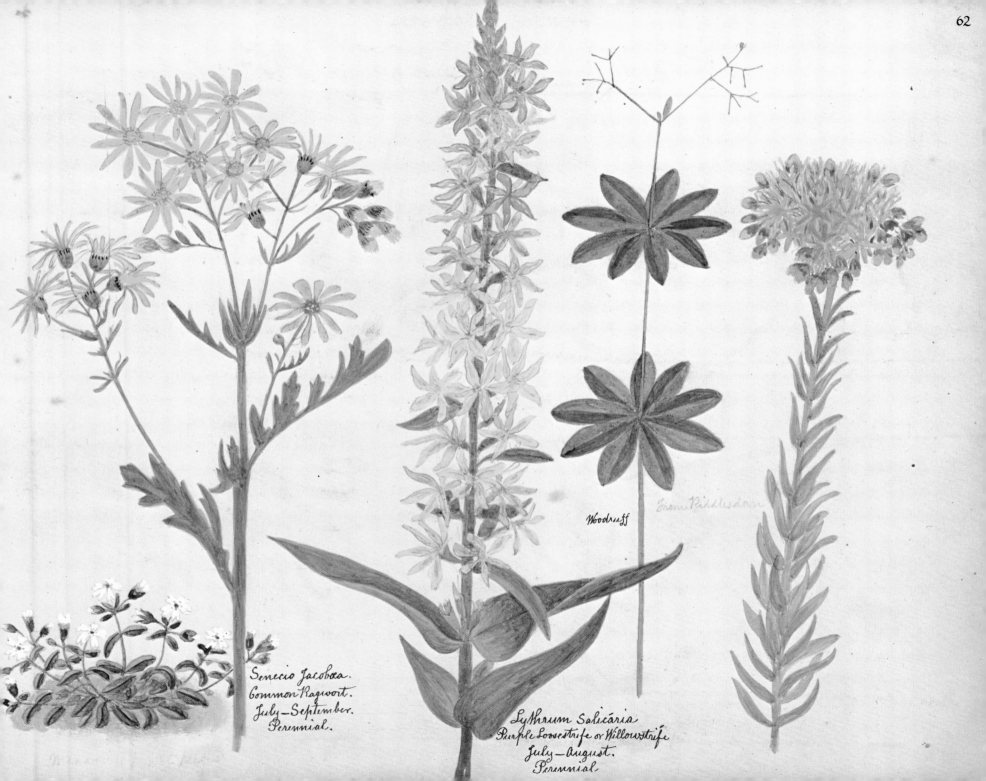

62

Senecio Jacobæa.
Common Ragwort.
July — September.
Perennial.

Woodruff

From Riddlesdown

Lythrum Salicaria
Purple Loosestrife or Willowstrife
July — August.
Perennial.

63

Medicāgo sativa
Lucerne
April–June
Annual

Hippocrepis Comosa.
Tufted Horse-shoe Vetch.
May–August.
Perennial.

Sneeze-wort

Erica cinerea.
Fine–leaved Heath.
July–August.
Shrub.

Anthemis nobilis.
Common Chamomile.
August–
Perennial.

Ballota nigra.
Black Horehound.
July—September.
Perennial.

Briza Media.
Quake-grass or Shakers.
May—July.
Perennial.

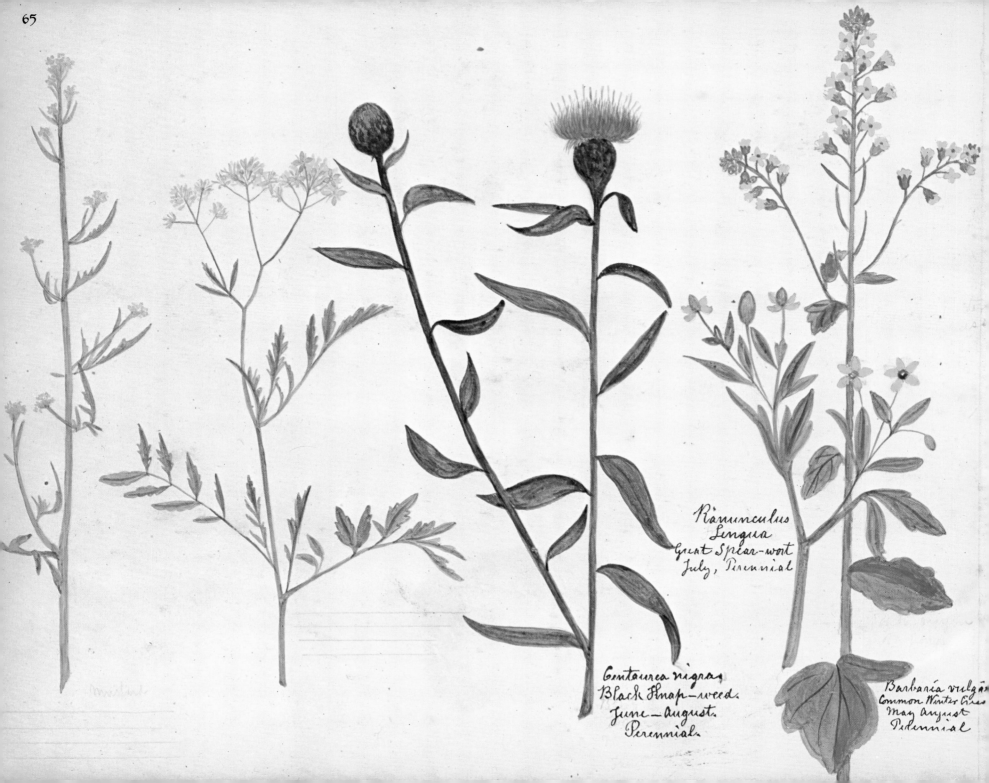

Ranunculus
Lingua
Great Spear-wort
July, Perennial

Centaurea nigra
Black Knap-weed.
June—August.
Perennial.

Barbaria vulgaris
Common Winter Cress
May August
Perennial

Dipsacus sylvestris.
Wild Teasel.
July—August.
Biennial.

ctium Lappa.
mmon Bur-dock.
July—August.
Biennial.

Carduus Marianus.
Milk Thistle.
June—July.
Biennial.

Origanum vulgàrē.
Common Marjoram.
July – August.
Perennial.

Cichorium Intybus.
Wild Chicory.
July.
Perennial.

Hypericum calycium.
Large flowered St John's wort.
July – September.
Perennial.

Sonchus oleraceus.
Common Sow-thistle
June – September
Annual.

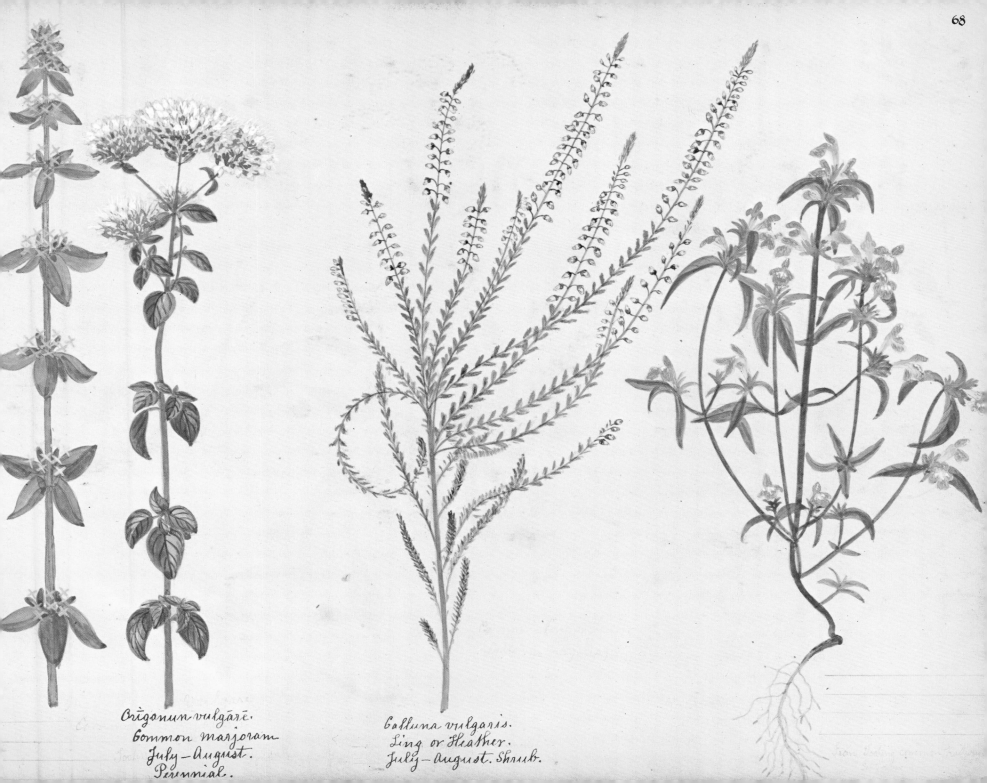

Origanun vulgare.
Common marjoram
July–August.
Perennial.

Calluna vulgaris.
Ling or Heather.
July–August. Shrub.

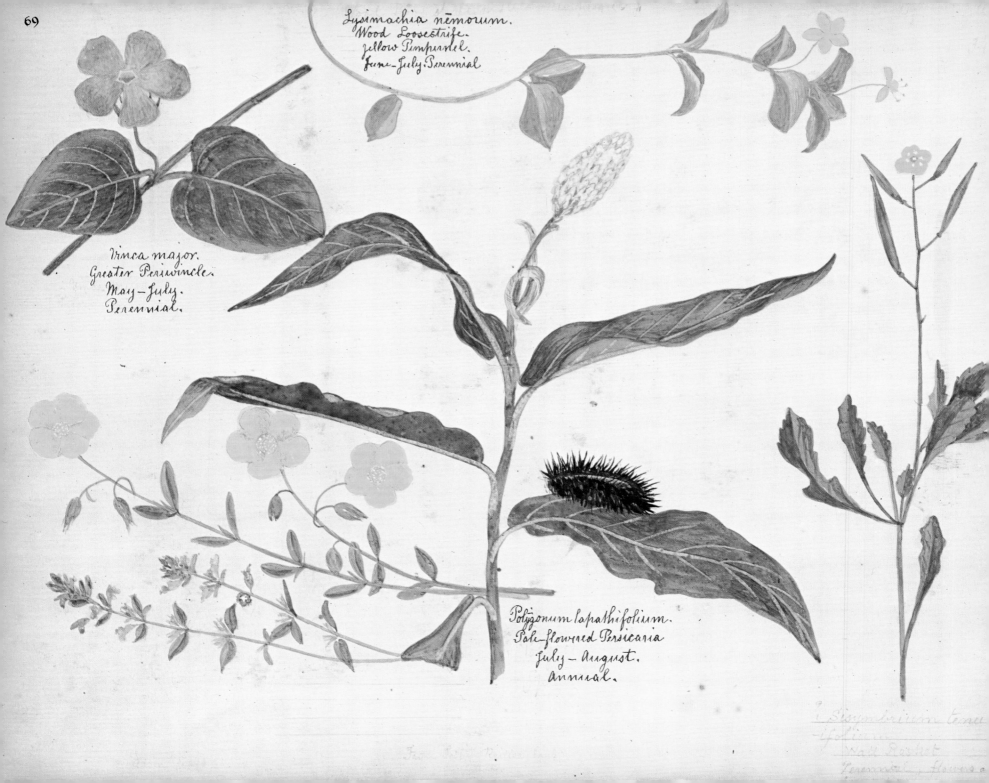

69

Lysimachia nemorum.
Wood Loosestrife.
Yellow Pimpernel.
June-July Perennial.

Vinca major.
Greater Periwinkle.
May-July.
Perennial.

Polygonum lapathifolium.
Pale-flowered Persicaria
July-August.
Annual.

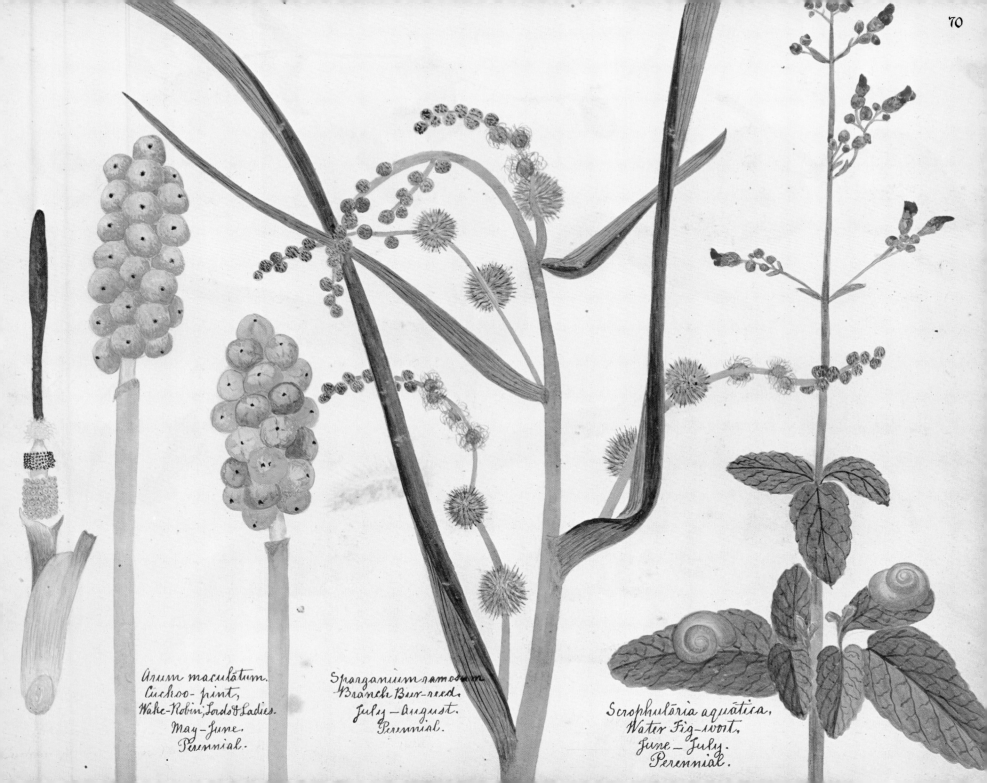

Arum maculatum.
Cuckoo-pint,
Wake-Robin, Lords & Ladies.
May–June.
Perennial.

Sparganium ramosum.
Branch Bur-reed.
July–August.
Perennial.

Scrophularia aquatica.
Water Fig-wort.
June–July.
Perennial.

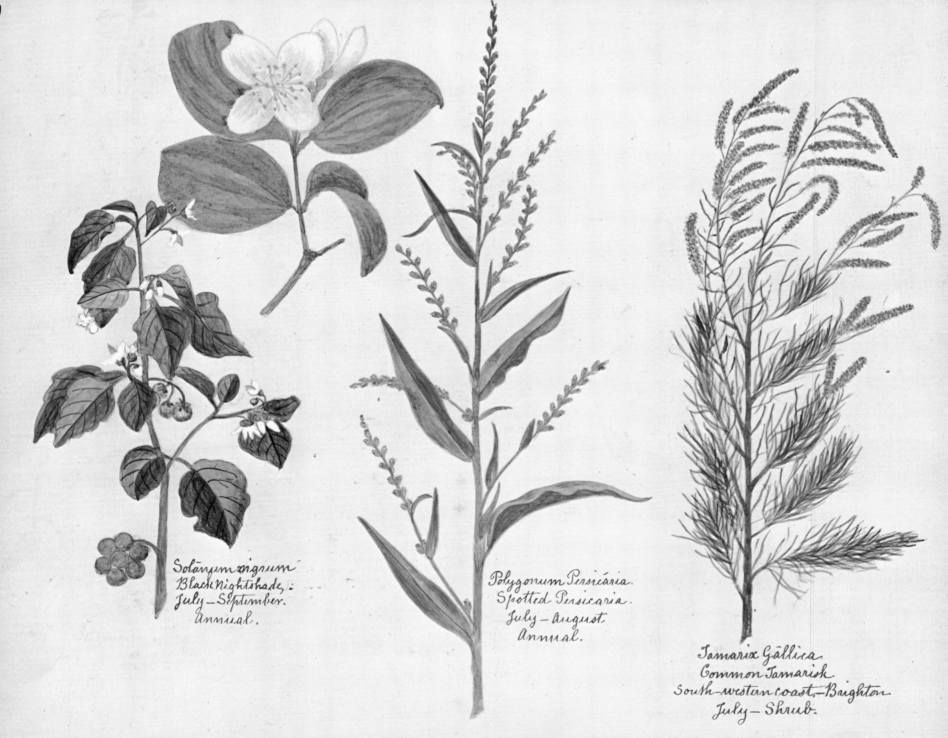

Solanum nigrum
Black Nightshade,
July — September.
Annual.

Polygonum Persicaria.
Spotted Persicaria.
July — August.
Annual.

Tamarix Gâllica
Common Tamarisk.
South-western coast.—Brighton
July — Shrub.

Hypericum perforatum.
Perforated S. John's Wort.
July — August
Perennial.

Ononis arvensis.
Rest-Harrow.
All the summer.
Perennial.

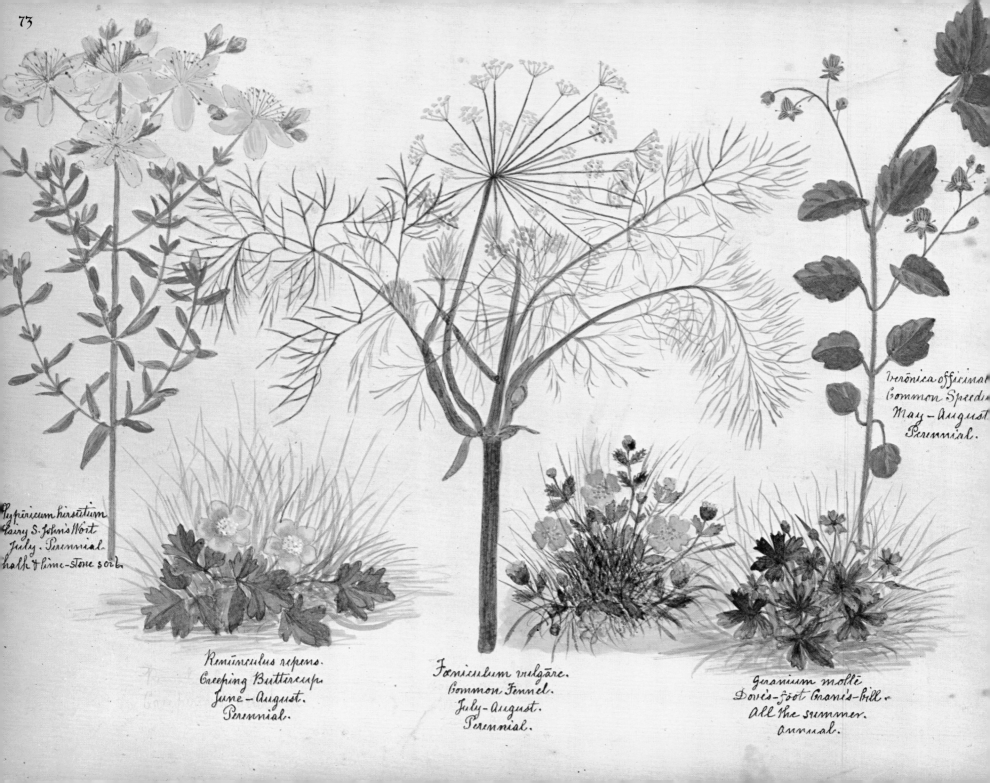

Hypericum hirsutum
Hairy S. John's Wort
July. Perennial.
chalk & lime-stone soil.

Ranunculus repens.
Creeping Buttercup.
June-August.
Perennial.

Fœniculum vulgare.
Common Fennel.
July-August.
Perennial.

Veronica officinal
Common Speedw
May-August.
Perennial.

Geranium molle
Dove's-foot Crane's-bill.
All the summer.
Annual.

Anagallis arvensis
Scarlet Pimpernel
Poor man's weather-glass.
Opens only in fine weather
June — July. Annual.

Agrostemma Githago.
Corn Cockle.
June — July.
Perennial.

Scutellaria galericulata.
Greater Skull — Cap.
July — September.
Perennial.

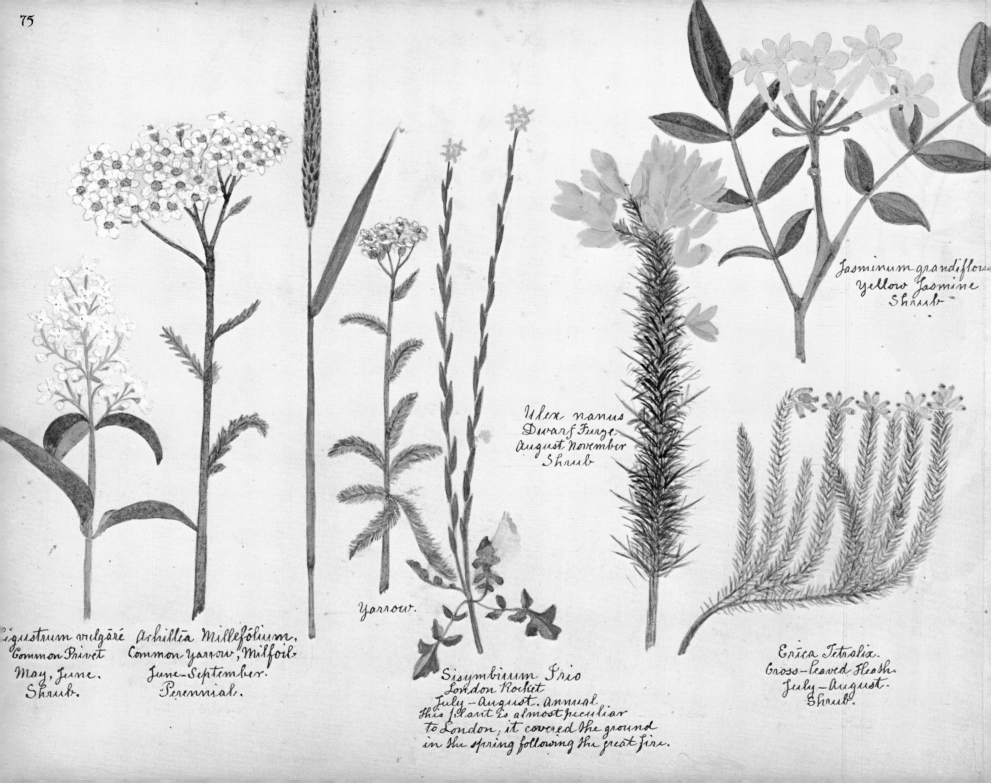

Jasminum grandiflorum
Yellow Jasmine
Shrub.

Ulex nanus
Dwarf Furze
August November
Shrub

Yarrow.

Ligustrum vulgäre
Common Privet
May, June.
Shrub.

Achillea Millefolium.
Common Yarrow, Milfoil.
June–September.
Perennial.

Sisymbrium Irio
London Rocket
July–August. Annual.
This plant is almost peculiar
to London, it covered the ground
in the spring following the great fire.

Erica Tetralix.
Cross-leaved Heath.
July–August.
Shrub.

S. Johns Wort.

St Johns Wort

Circæa Lutetiana.
Common Enchanter's Nightshade.
July — August. Perennial.

Arbutus Unedo
Strawberry-tree
September, October
Tree

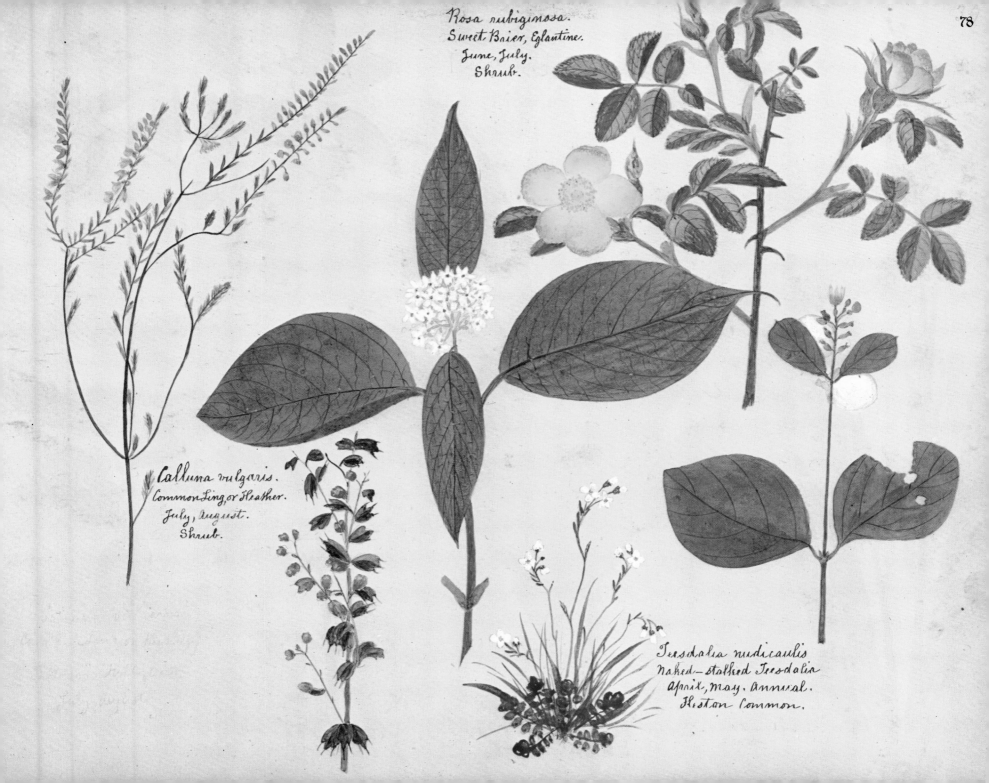

Rosa rubiginosa.
Sweet Brier, Eglantine.
June, July.
Shrub.

Calluna vulgaris.
Common Ling or Heather.
July, August.
Shrub.

Teesdalia nudicaulis
Naked-stalked Teesdalia
April, May. Annual.
Heston Common.

nvallaria majalis.
illy of the Valley.
May.
Perennial.

Oxalis Acetosella.
Common Wood-Sorrel.
May, June.

Milkwort.
Polygala vulgaris

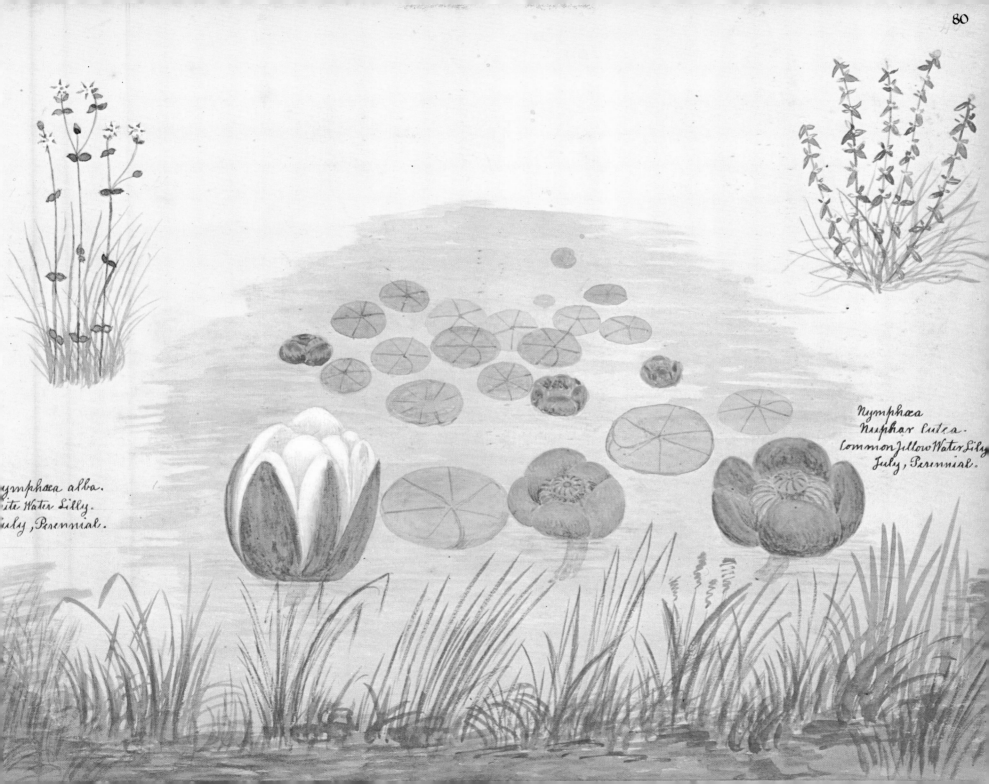

Nymphæa
Nuphar lutea.
Common Jellow Water Lily.
July, Perennial.

ymphæa alba.
ite Water Lilly.
uly, Perennial.

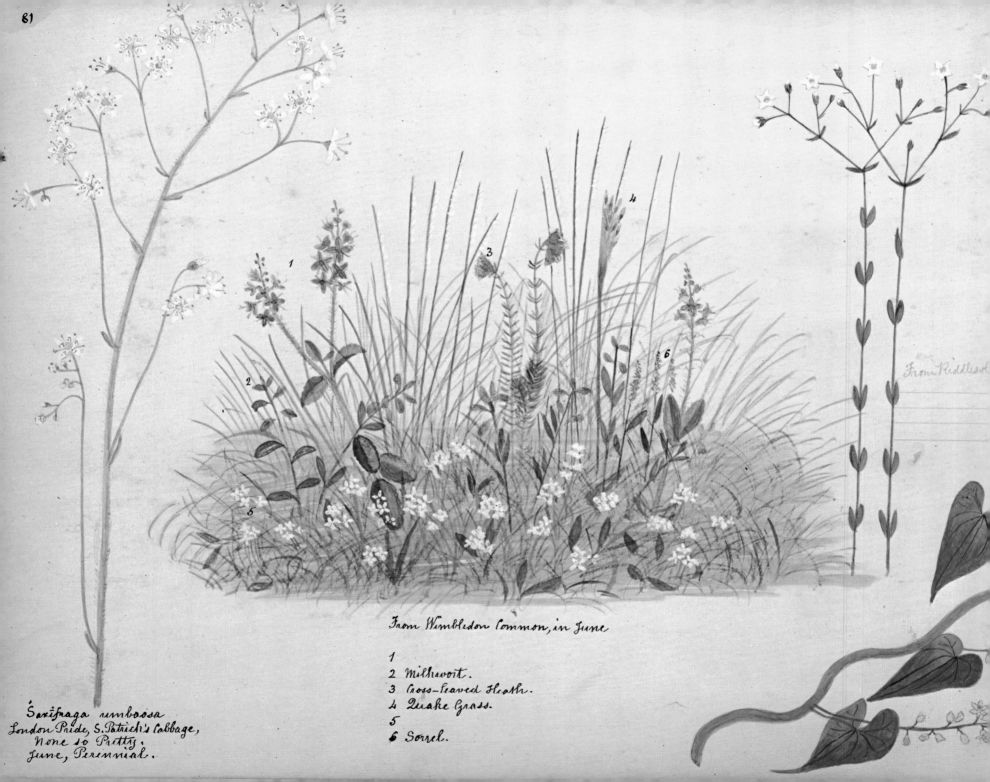

From Wimbledon Common, in June

1
2 Milkwort.
3 Cross-leaved Heath.
4 Quake Grass.
5
6 Sorrel.

Saxifraga umbrosa
London Pride, S. Patrick's Cabbage,
None so Pretty.
June, Perennial.

From Riddlesdown

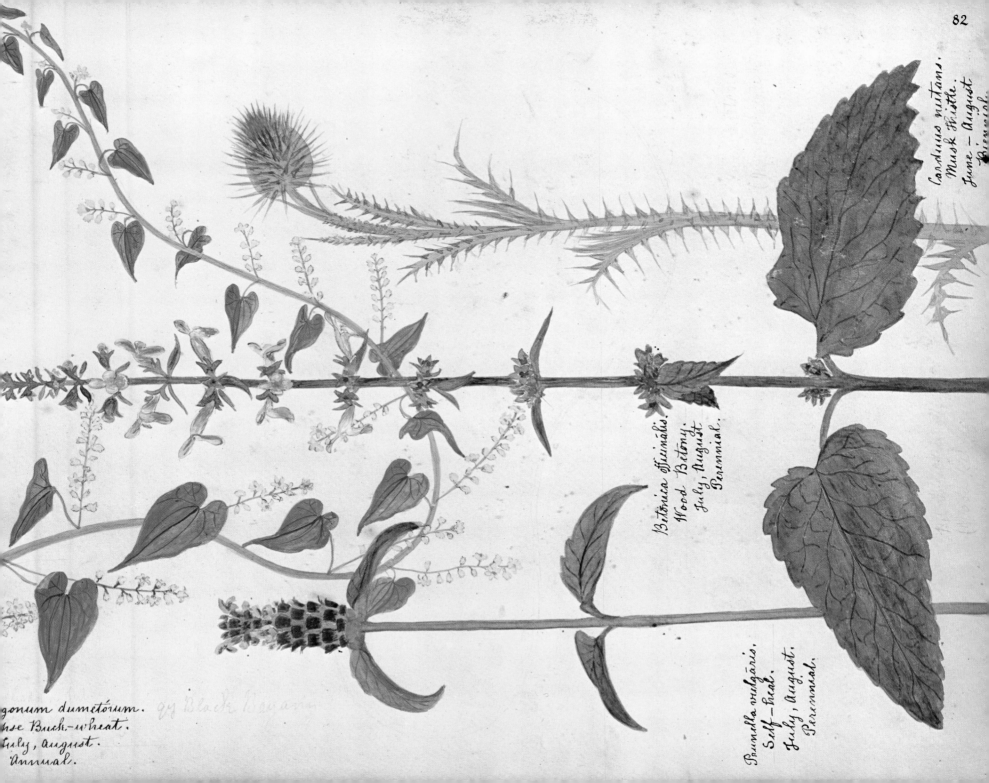

Carduus nutans.
Musk Thistle.
June — August
Biennial.

Betonica officinalis.
Wood Betony.
July, August.
Perennial.

Prunella vulgaris.
Self — heal.
July, August.
Perennial.

gonum dumetorum.
hse Buck.-wheat.
July, August.
Annual.

gg Black Bayary

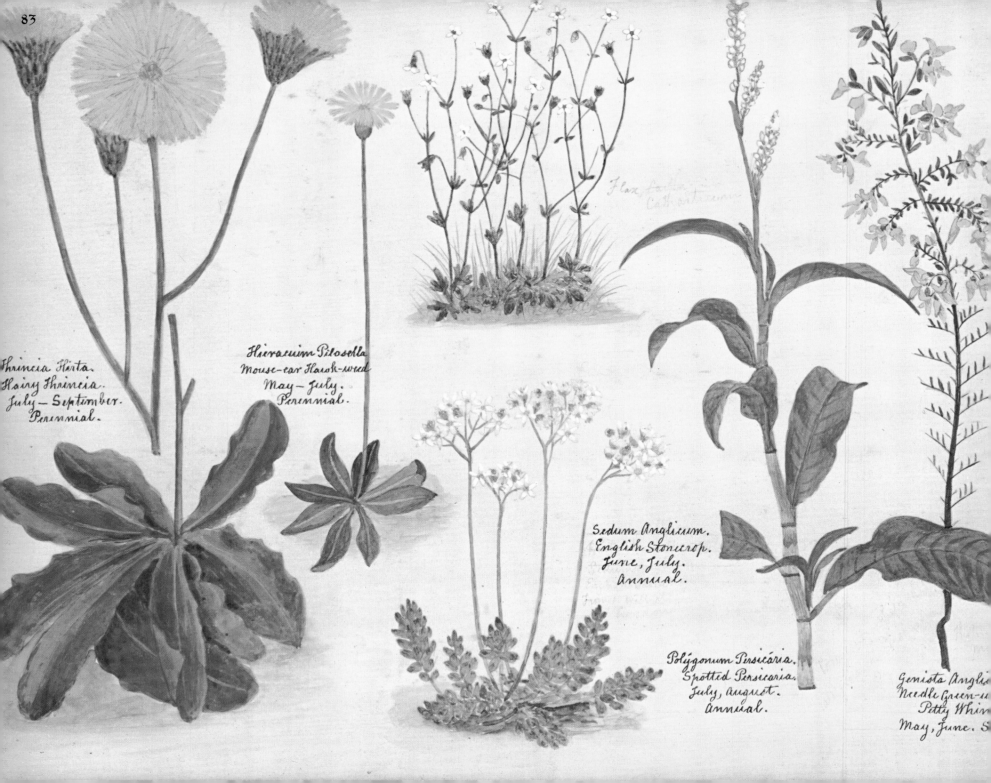

Thrincia Hirta.
Hairy Thrincia.
July – September.
Perennial.

Hieracium Pilosella.
Mouse-ear Hawk-weed.
May – July.
Perennial.

Flax bastard
Catharticum

Sedum Anglicum.
English Stonecrop.
June, July.
Annual.

Polygonum Persicaria.
Spotted Persicaria.
July, August.
Annual.

Genista Anglica.
Needle Green-weed
Petty Whin.
May, June. S

Wheat

Wheat

Papaver
Long Smooth-
June, July.
Annual.

Dubium.
headed Poppy.

Convolvulus
arvensis
Field Bindweed
June, July.
Perennial.

Barley

Papaver
Common
June

Rhœa,
Red Poppy.
July.
Annual.

Meconopsis Cambrica.
Yellow Welsh Poppy.
June, July.
Perennial.

85

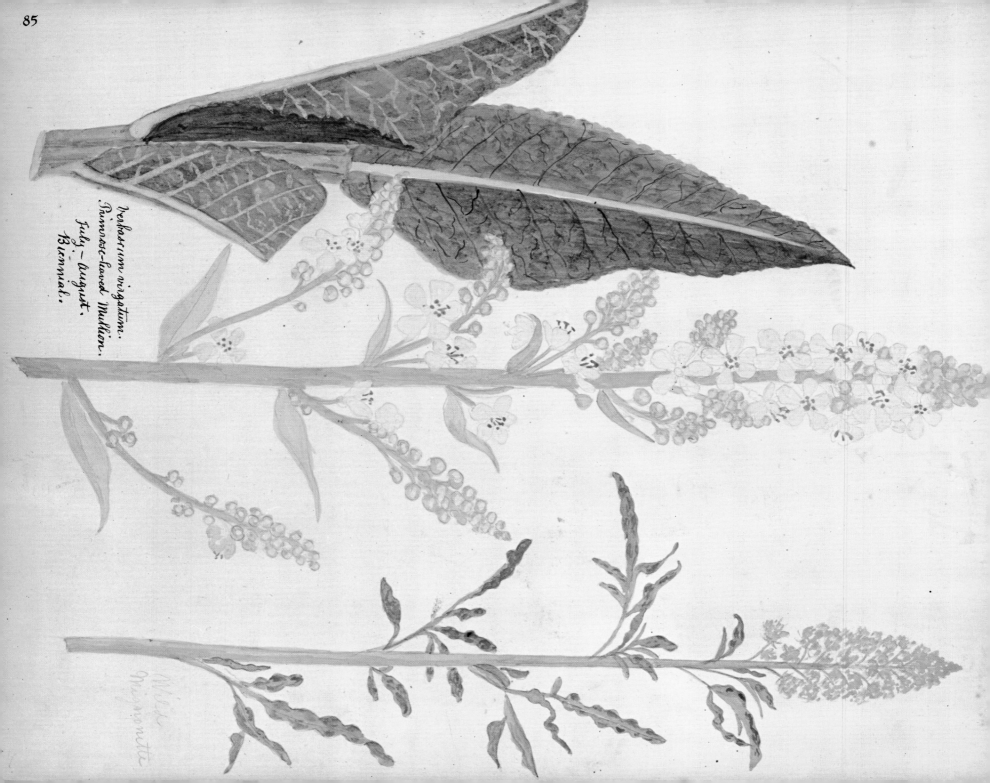

Verbascum virgatum.
Primrose-leaved Mullein.
July – August.
Biennial.

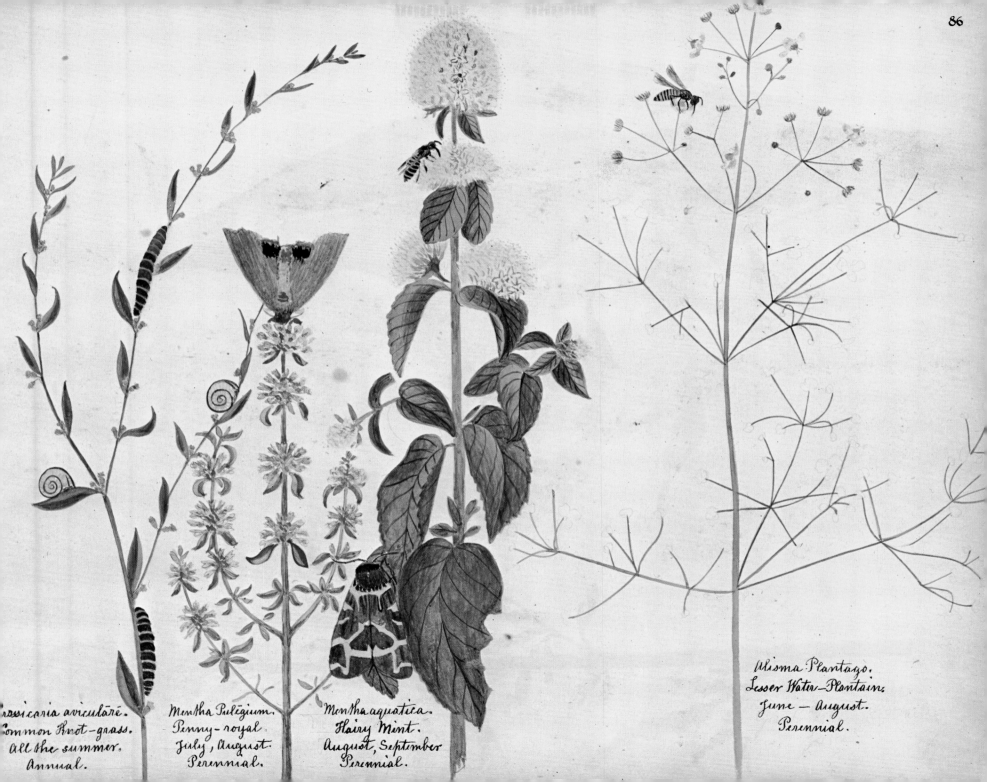

Polygonaria aviculare.
Common Knot-grass.
All the summer.
Annual.

Mentha Pulegium.
Penny-royal.
July, August.
Perennial.

Mentha aquatica.
Hairy Mint.
August, September.
Perennial.

Alisma Plantago.
Lesser Water-Plantain.
June — August.
Perennial.

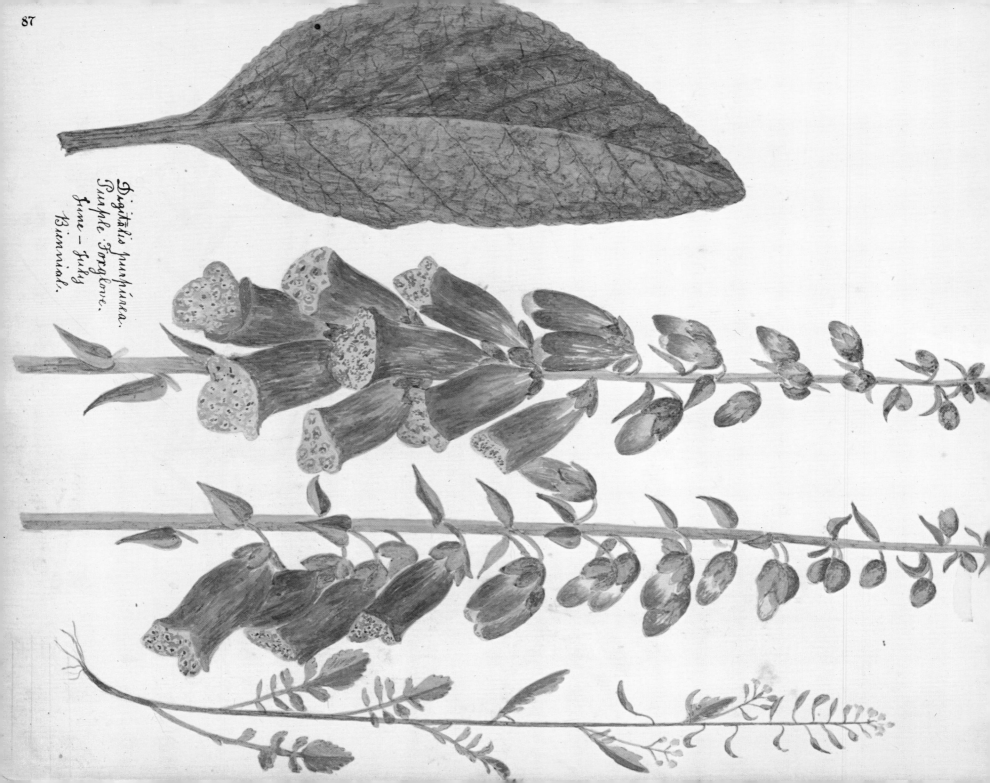

Digitalis purpurea.
Purple Foxglove.
June — July.
Biennial.

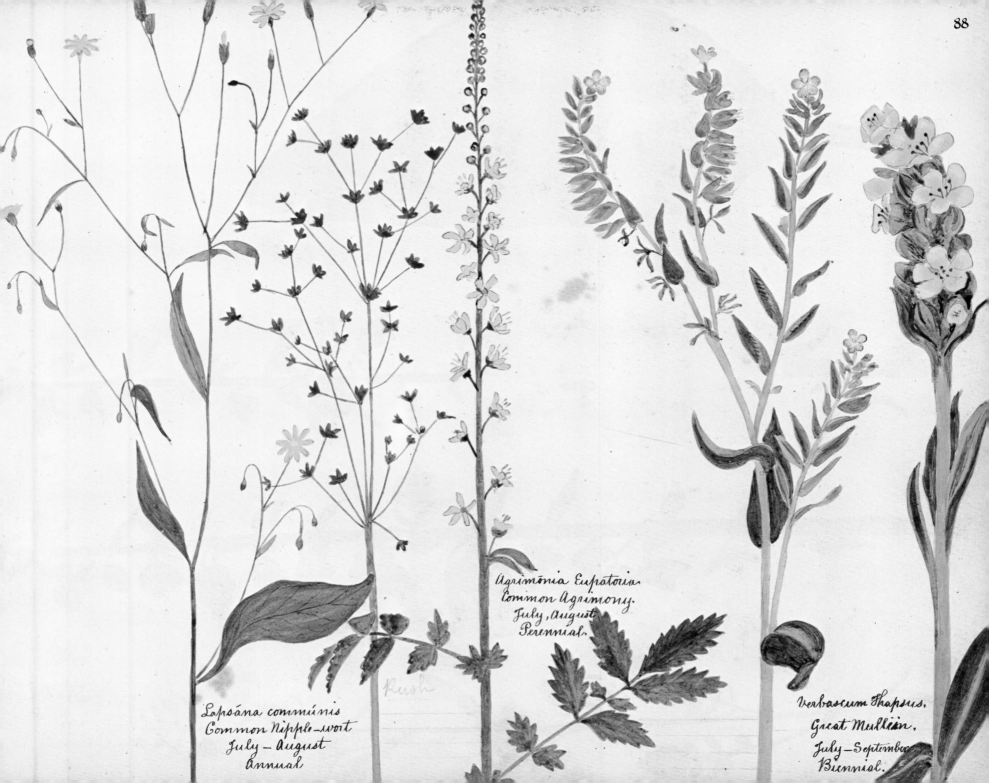

Agrimónia Eupatoria
Common Agrimony.
July, August
Perennial.

Lapsána commúnis
Common Nipple-wort
July – August
Annual

Verbascum Thapsus.
Great Mullein.
July – September
Biennial.

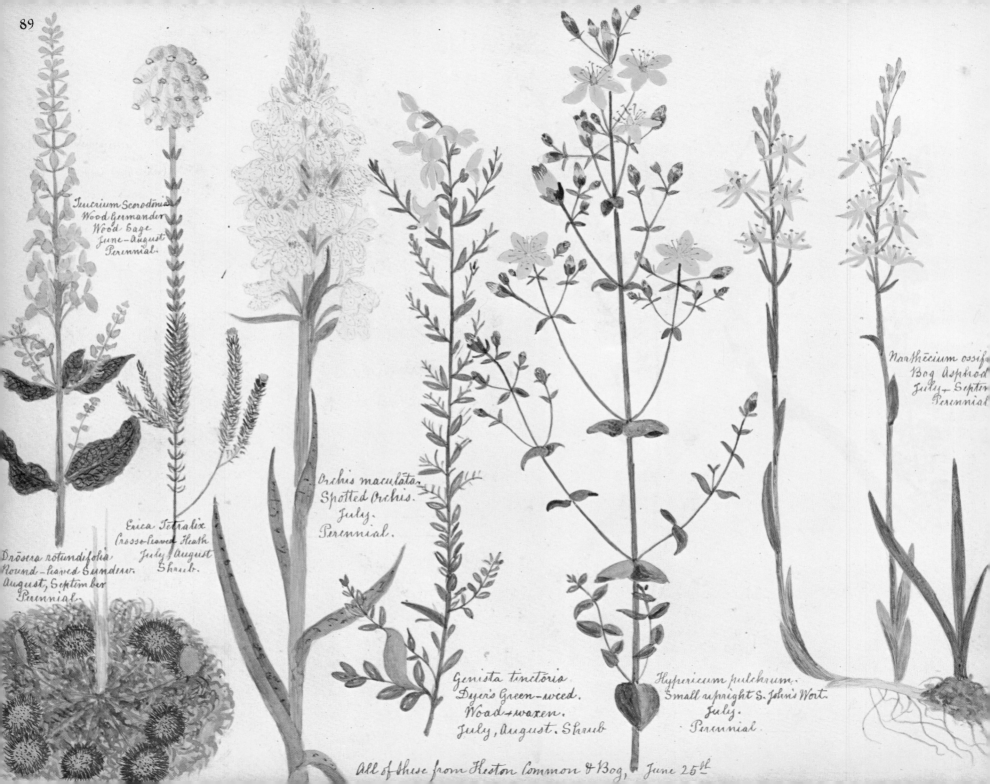

89

Teucrium Scorodonia
Wood Germander
Wood Sage
June – August
Perennial.

Erica Tetralix
Cross-leaved Heath
July, August
Shrub.

Drosera rotundifolia
Round-leaved Sundew.
August, September
Perennial.

Orchis maculata.
Spotted Orchis.
July.
Perennial.

Genista tinctoria
Dyer's Green-weed.
Woad-waxen.
July, August. Shrub

Hypericum pulchrum.
Small upright S. John's Wort.
July.
Perennial.

Narthecium ossifr
Bog Asphod
July – Septem
Perennial.

All of these from Heston Common & Bog, June 25th

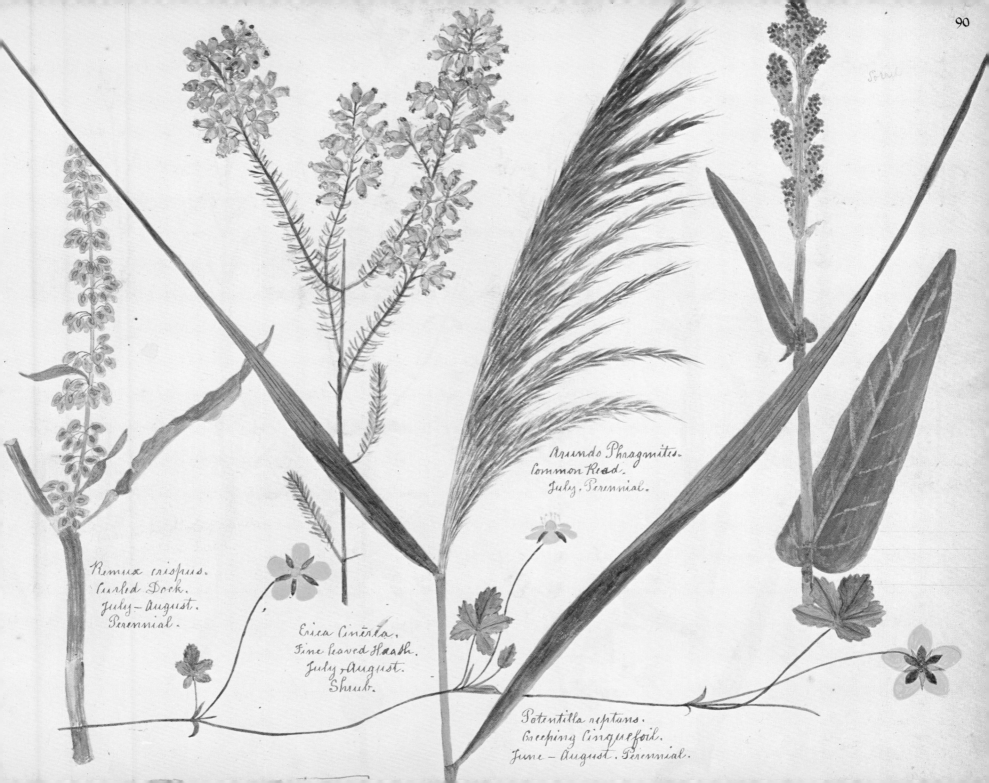

Soleil

Arundo Phragmites.
Common Reed.
July. Perennial.

Rumex crispus.
Curled Dock.
July - August.
Perennial.

Erica Cinerea.
Fine leaved Heath.
July - August.
Shrub.

Potentilla reptans.
Creeping Cinquefoil.
June - August. Perennial.

91

Tilia europæa
Lime or London tree

Rosa Rubiginosa.
Sweet Brier.
June, July.
Shrub.

Matricaria Parthenium.
Common Feverfew.
July, August.
Perennial.

Campanula glomerata
Clustered Bell-flower.
July August.
Perennial.

Lycopsis arvensis.
Small Bugloss.
June—August.
Annual.

Rumex Acetosella.
Sheep's Sorrell.
May—July. Perennial.

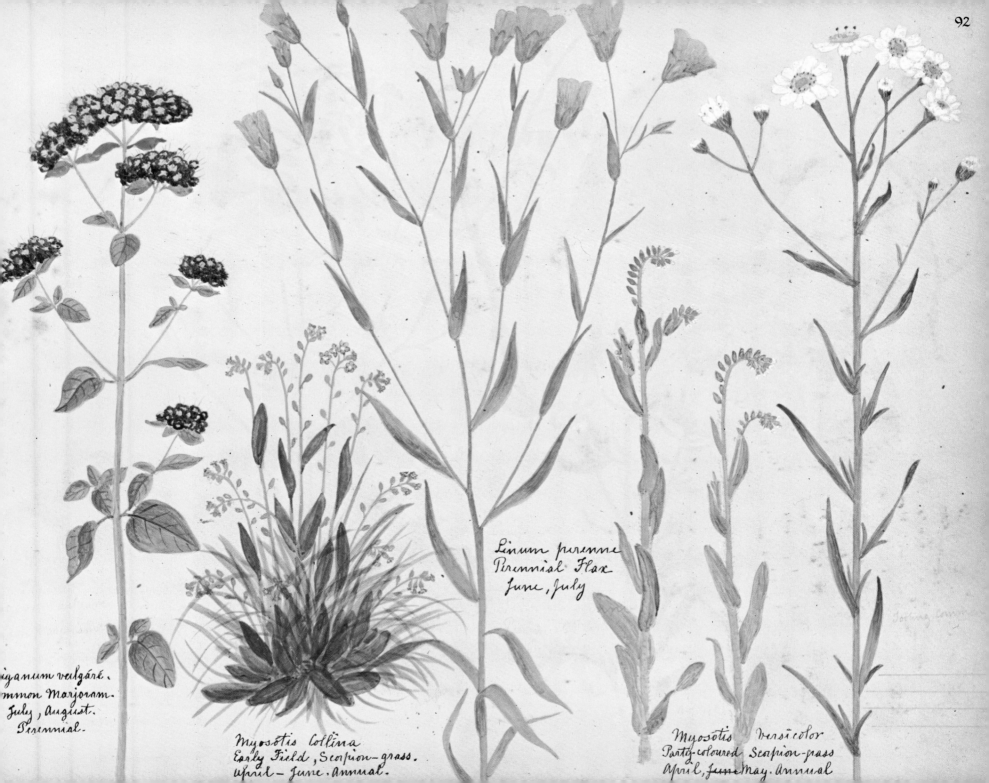

Origanum vulgāré.
Common Marjoram.
July, August.
Perennial.

Myosotis collina
Early Field, Scorpion-grass.
April – June. Annual.

Linum perenne
Perennial Flax
June, July

Myosotis versicolor
Partly-coloured Scorpion-grass
April, June May. Annual

Cnicus palustris
Marsh Plume-Thistle
July, August
Biennial.

Drosera rotundifolia
Sundew
July, August
Perennial.

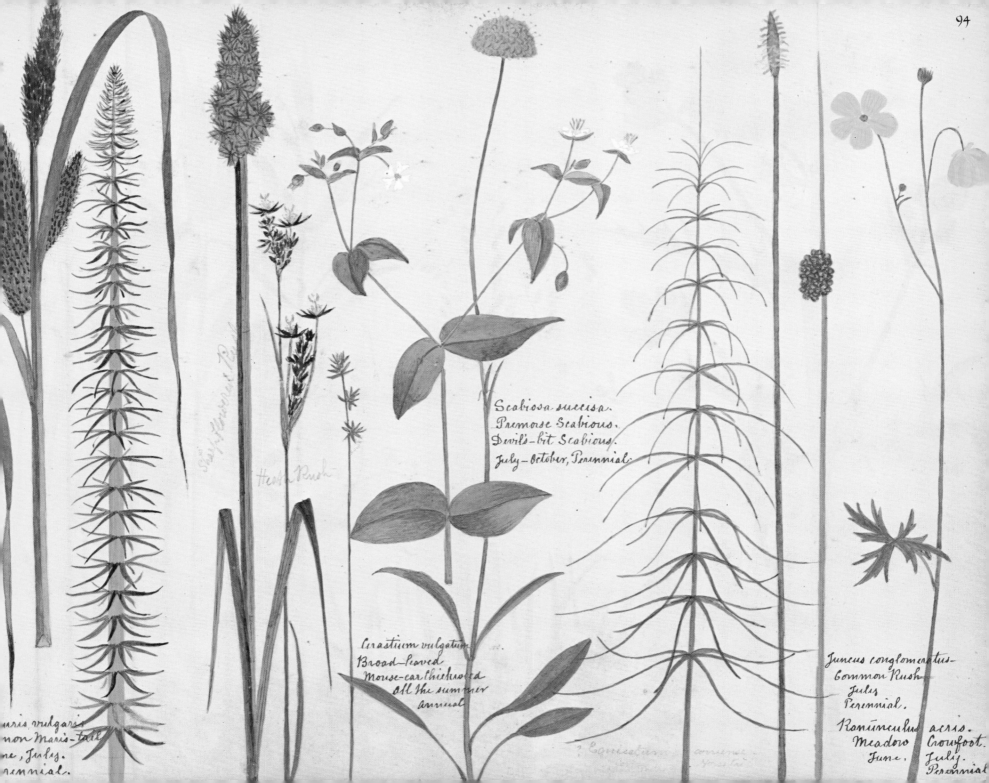

Sheep's-fescue Rush

Heath Rush

Scabiosa succisa.
Premorse Scabious.
Devil's-bit Scabious.
July–October, Perennial.

Cerastium vulgatum
Broad-leaved
Mouse-ear Chickweed
All the summer
Annual

? Equisetum arvense

Juncus conglomeratus.
Common Rush
July.
Perennial.

Ranunculus acris.
Meadow Crowfoot.
June. July.
Perennial.

...ris vulgaris
non Maris-tail
ne, July.
Perennial.

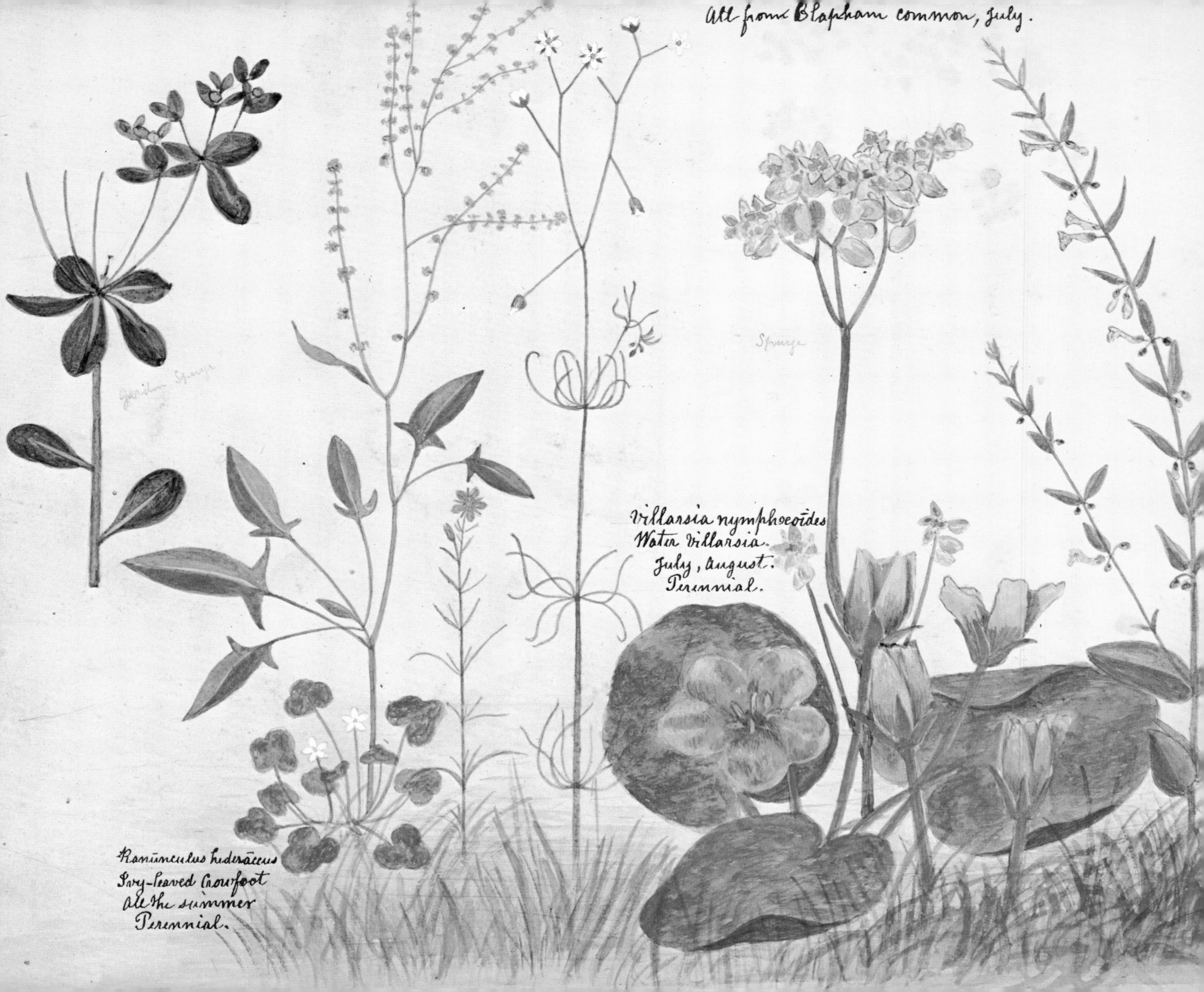

All from Clapham common, July.
Garden Spurge
Spurge
Villarsia nymphoeoides
Water Villarsia.
July, August.
Perennial.
Ranunculus hederaceus
Ivy-leaved Crowfoot
All the summer
Perennial.

Grass of Parnassus
Enlarged 3 times

Chærophyllum
sylvestre.

Parnassia palustris.
Common Grass of
Parnassus. August —
October. Perennial.

Harebell

Phyteuma orbiculare
Round-headed Rampion
July.
Perennial.

Verbena officinalis.
Common Vervain.
July August
Perennial.

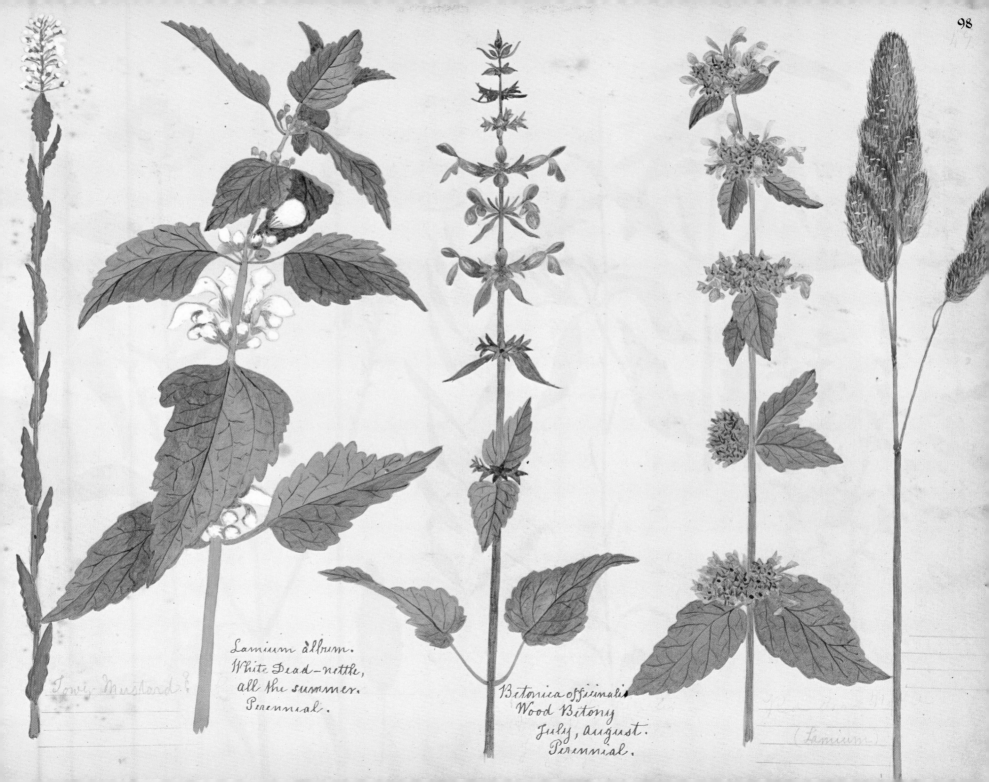

Tower Mustard?

Lamium àlbum.
White Dead-nettle,
all the summer.
Perennial.

Betonica officinalis
Wood Betony
July, August.
Perennial.

(Lamium)

Verbascum Thapsus.
Great Mullein.
July, August.
Biennial.
from Riddlesdown.

Verbascum nigrum
Dark Mullein.
July-September.
Biennial.
from Riddlesdown

Orobanche minor.
Fig Orobie
May & June

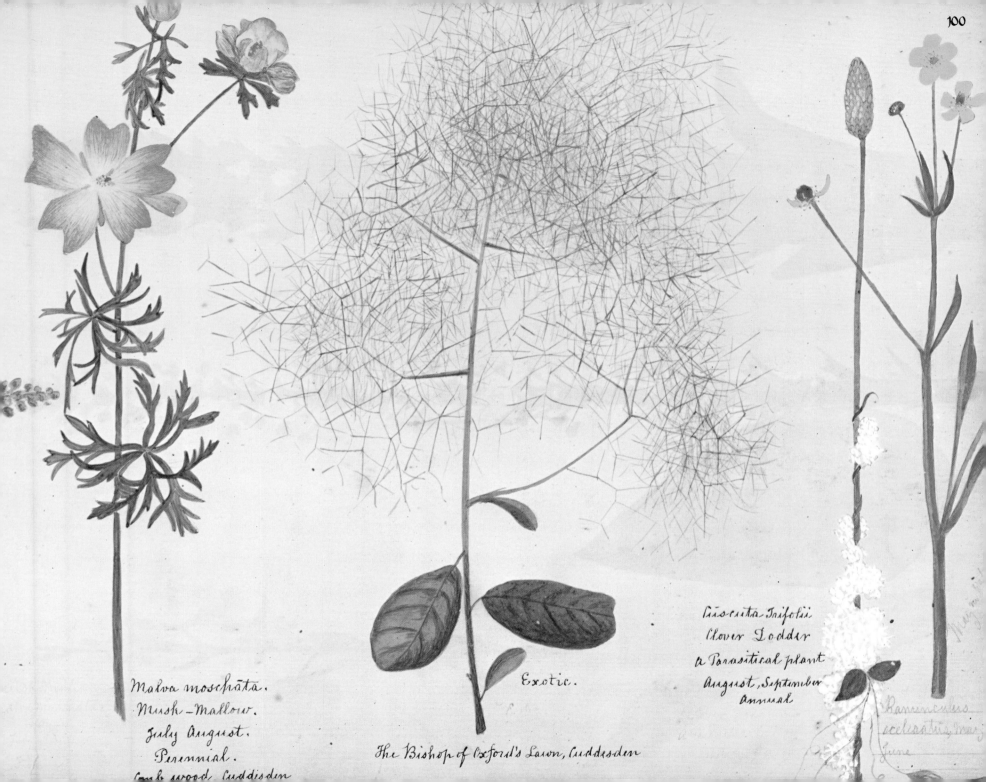

Malva moschata.

Musk-Mallow.

July August.

Perennial.

Cuck wood, Cuddesden

The Bishop of Oxford's Lawn, Cuddesden

Exotic.

Cuscuta Trifolii

Clover Dodder

a Parasitical plant

August, September

Annual

Ranunculus

acrlaceus, May

June

Buck-wheat

Lycopus Europœus.
Common Gipsy-wort.
July, August. Perennial.

Lysimachia num
Money-wort, Herb-t
Creeping Jenny.
June, July, Perenn

Colchicum autumnale.
Meadow Saffron.
September, October.
Perennial.

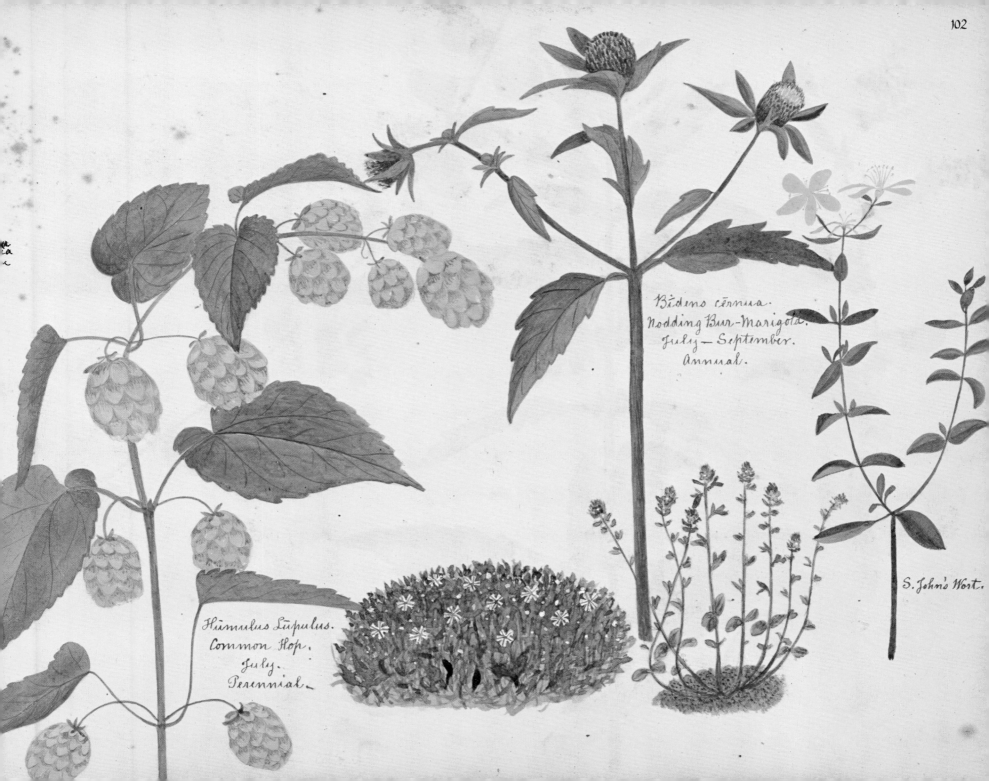

Bidens cernua.
Nodding Bur-Marigold.
July — September.
Annual.

Humulus Lupulus.
Common Hop.
July.
Perennial.

S. John's Wort.

103

Orchis mascula
Early purple Orchis.
May, June. Perennial.

Habenaria bifolia
Butterfly Orchis
June. Perennial
Fragrant in the evening

Aceras
anthropophora
Green Man Orchis
June July
Perennial

Gymnadenia conopsea
Sweet scented Orchis
June, July.
Perennial.

Orchis latifolia
Marsh Orchis.
June, July.
Perennial.

Orchis
maculata
Spotted Orchis
June July
Perennial

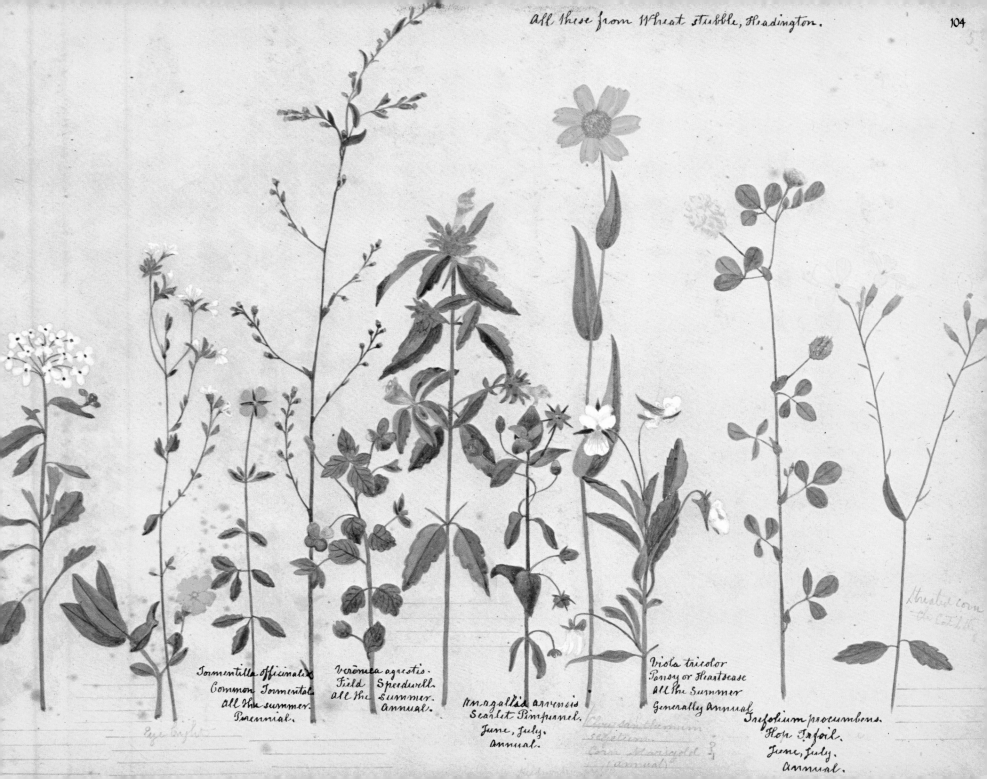

Tormentilla officinalis.
Common Tormentil.
All the summer.
Perennial.

Veronica agrestis.
Field Speedwell.
All the summer.
Annual.

Anagallis arvensis.
Scarlet Pimpernel.
June, July.
Annual.

Chrysanthemum
segetum.
Corn Marigold ?
(annual)

Viola tricolor
Pansy or Heartsease
All the Summer
Generally Annual.

Trifolium procumbens.
Hop Trefoil.
June, July.
Annual.

Eye Bright

Polemōnium cœruleum
Greek Valerian
Blue Jacobs Ladder
June, July. Perennial.

mountain
Groundsell
95

St Mary Gray
June

Antirrhinum majus.
Great Snapdragon.
June - August.
Perennial.

Silene

Co

Arctium Lappa.
Common Bur-dock.
July. August.
Biennial.

Solanum Tuberosum.
Potato
July, August

Mountain Groundsel ?
99
Off pavel Heston Common

Lactuca muralis
Ivy leaved Lettuce
July September
Biennial

Cnicus acaulis. Dwarf Plume-Thistle.
July, August. Perennial.

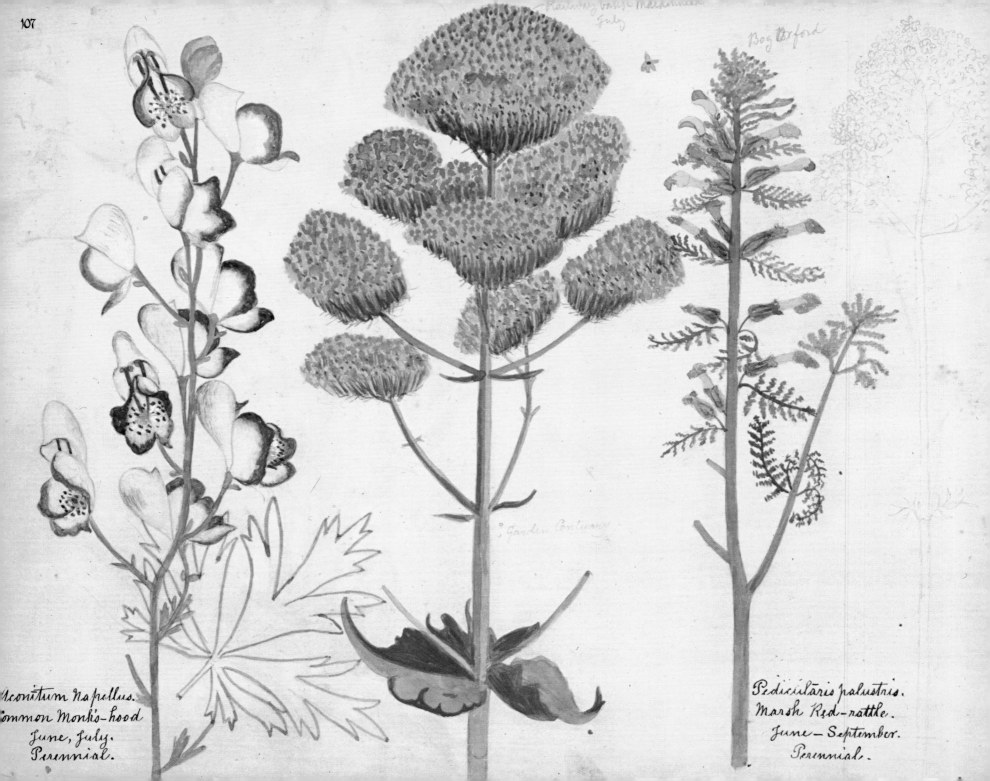

Aconitum Napellus.
Common Monk's-hood.
June, July.
Perennial.

Pedicularis palustris.
Marsh Red-rattle.
June—September.
Perennial.

Bog Oxford

Potentilla reptans.
Creeping Cinquefoil
June—August. Perennial

Matricaria inodora.
Corn Feverfew;
Scentless May-weed.
July—October. Annual.

anicula Europœa
Wood Sanicle.
une, July.
Perennial.

Ajuga reptans, Common Bugle
May June Perennial.

Bog Moss (Sphagnum)
Heston Bog, May.

Saxifraga gran
White Saxifr

…a Ulmaria
…ow—sweet
…ly, August
…erennial

…vulgāris
Lysimachia ~~nemorum~~
Great Yellow Loosestrife
July, Perennial

Solidāgo Virgaūre…
Golden—rod
July, Septem…
Perennial

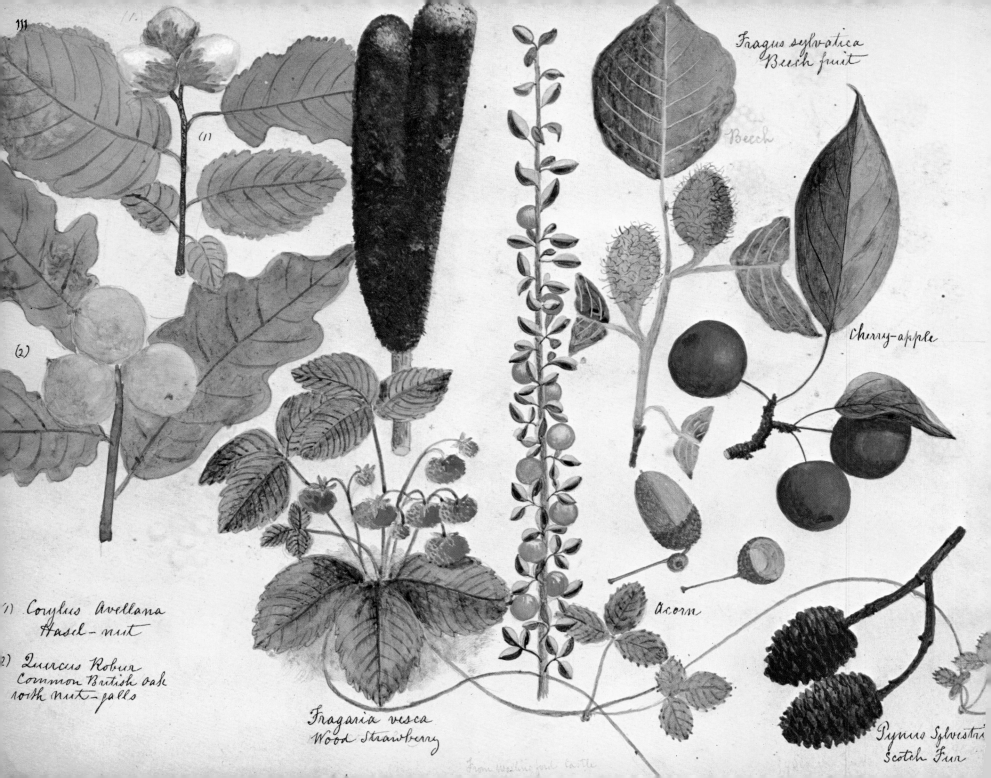

111

(1)

(2)

1) Corylus Avellana
   Hasel-nut

2) Quercus Robur
   Common British Oak
   with nut-galls

Fragaria vesca
Wood Strawberry

Fagus sylvatica
Beech fruit

Beech

Cherry-apple

Acorn

Pinus Sylvestris
Scotch Fir

From Wallingford Castle

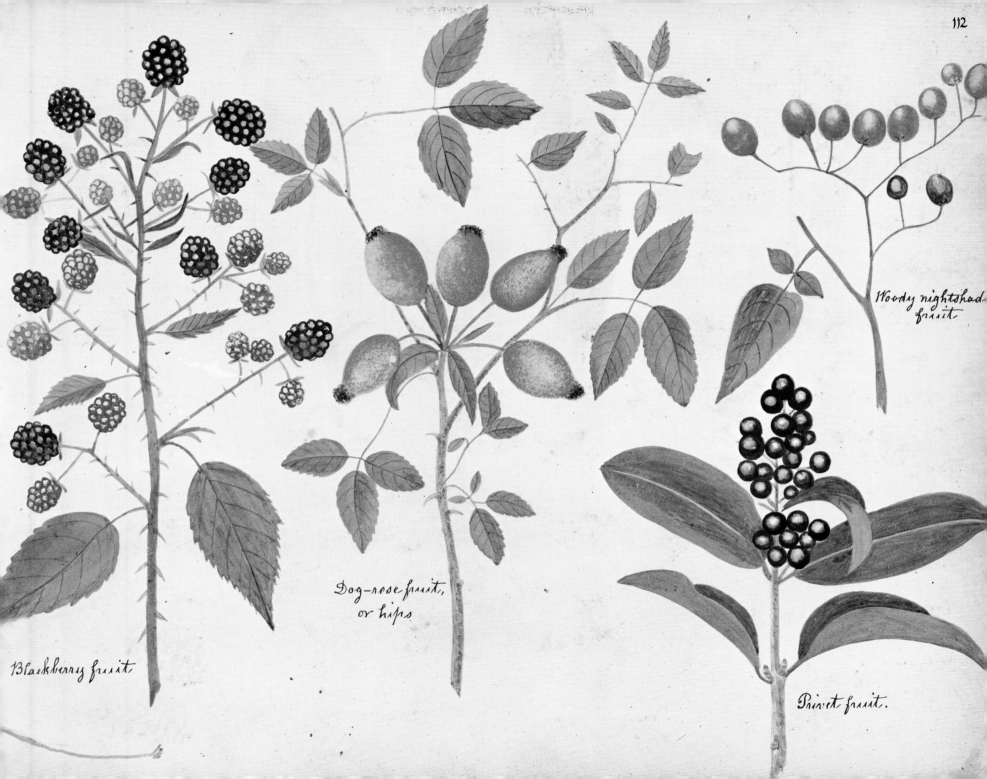

112

Woody nightshade fruit.

Dog-rose fruit, or hips

Blackberry fruit

Privet fruit.

113

"O Father Lord!
The All-beneficent! I bless Thy name
That Thou hast mantled the green earth with flowers
Linking our hearts to nature! By the love
Of their wild blossoms our young footsteps first
Into her deep recesses are beguiled."

"By the breath of flowers
Thou callest us, from city throng and cares;
Back to the woods, the birds, the mountain streams,
That sing of Thee!"

"Thou bidd'st
The lillies of the field with placid smile
Reprove man's feverish strivings, and infuse
Through his warm soul a more unworldly life,
With their soft holy breath."

"Receive
Thanks, blessings, love for these Thy lavish boons,
Aad most of all their heavenward influences;
Oh Thou that gavest us flowers."

MRS. HEMANS.

LIST OF FLOWERS AND INSECTS ILLUSTRATED

The scientific and English names of the flowers have been quoted, as far as possible, from *English Names of Wild Flowers*, by J. G. Dony, C. M. Rob and F. H. Perring, published by Butterworths in 1974. This is a recommended standard list of names. If it has proved impossible to name a flower with certainty, a question mark has been put beside the name, or else sp. which is short for species. Sometimes the name given by Henry Terry has been accepted, even though the flower could belong to some similar species, although it is not possible to tell. The names have been listed from left to right, and then from top to bottom, in the cases where there is more than one row of paintings per page. Under status, W stands for wild, N for naturalised i.e. not wild in the first place, but now behaving as if it were wild, and G for any garden plant. Under common, C stands for common, L for local (neither common nor rare, or only common in some places), and R for rare. How common a plant is may be a matter of opinion, according to where in the country one lives. The notes given only apply to wild or naturalised species. This information refers to modern times, and may have been different a hundred years ago e.g. Corncockle, p. 74, is rare now, but was common then.

Richard Pankhurst (Department of Botany) named the flowers, and Paul Whalley (Department of Entomology) named the insects.

R.P., P.W., British Museum (Natural History)

	Scientific name	English name	Status	Common
page 2	Genista sp.		G	
	Primula 'polyanthus'		G	
	Caltha palustris	Marsh Marigold	W	C
	Crocus flavus (2)	Yellow Crocus	G	
	Crocus ?purpureus	Spring Crocus	G, N	R
3	Taraxacum officinale (in seed)	Dandelion	W	C
	Forsythia		G	
	Ribes sanguineum (in bud)	Flowering Currant	G, N	L
	Ribes sanguineum (in flower)	Flowering Currant	G, N	L
	Taraxacum officinale (in flower)	Dandelion	W	C
	Ranunculus ficaria	Lesser Celandine	W	C
	Senecio vulgaris	Groundsel	W	C
	Erophila verna	Common Whitlow-grass	W	C
4	Lamium purpureum	Red Dead-nettle	W	C
	Lamium maculatum	Spotted Dead-nettle	G, N	L
	Eranthis hyemalis	Winter Aconite	G, N	L
	Galanthus nivalis	Snowdrop	G, N	C
	Tussilago farfara	Colt's-foot	W	C
	Anemone nemorosa	Wood Anemone	W	C
5	Ribes ?aureum	Golden Currant	G	
	Chaenomales japonica	Japonica	G	
	Capsella bursa-pastoris	Shepherd's-purse	W	C
	Mercurialis perennis	Dog's Mercury	W	C
	Glechoma hederacea	Ground-ivy	W	C
	Fragaria vesca	Wild Strawberry	W	C
	Adoxa moschatellina	Moschatel	W	L

	Scientific name	English name	Status	Common
page 6	Vinca minor	Lesser Periwinkle	N	L
	Corylus avellana	Hazel	W	C
	Senecio cruentus	Cineraria	G	
	Salix cinerea	Grey Willow	W	C
	Pulmonaria longifolia	Narrow-leaved Lungwort	W, G	R
	Ulex europaeus	Gorse	W	C
	Glechoma hederacea	Ground-ivy	W	C
	Viola odorata	Sweet Violet	W, G	C
	with Inachis io	Peacock Butterfly	W	C
7	Populus ? x canadensis (catkins)	Italian Poplar	G, N	C
	Galium aparine	Cleavers	W	C
	Plantago ?lanceolata	Ribwort Plantain	W	C
	Cerastium holosteoides	Common Mouse-ear	W	C
	Primula vulgaris	Primrose	W	C
8	Mahonia sp.		G	
	Primula veris	Cowslip	W	L
	Bellis perennis	Daisy	W	C
	Dianthus sp. (in bud)	Pink	G	
	Cardamine pratensis	Cuckooflower	W	C
9	Euphorbia ?peplus	Petty Spurge	W	C
	Caltha palustris	Marsh Marigold	W	C
	Ranunculus auricomus	Goldilocks Buttercup	W	L
	Alliaria petiolata	Garlic Mustard	W	C
	Euphorbia amygdaloides	Wood Spurge	W	C
10	Fritillaria meleagris	Fritillary	W, G	R

page	Scientific name	English name	Status	Common
page 11	?Malus sylvestris	Apple	G	-
	Aesculus hippocastanum	Horse Chestnut	G, N	C
	Morchella esculenta	Edible Morel	W	L
	Petasites hybridus	Butterbur	W	L
	?Erophila verna	Common Whitlow-grass	W	C
12	Anemone nemorosa	Wood Anemone	W	C
	Alliaria petiolata	Garlic Mustard	W	C
	Ribes sanguineum	Flowering Currant	G, N	L
	Senecio squalidus	Oxford Ragwort	N	C
	Endymion non-scriptus	Bluebell	W	C
	Malus sylvestris	Apple	G	-
13	Lithospermum arvense	Field Gromwell	W	L
	Glechoma hederacea	Ground-ivy	W	C
	Lamium purpureum	Red Dead-nettle	W	C
	Veronica hederifolia	Ivy-leaved Speedwell	W	C
	Stellaria holostea	Greater Stitchwort	W	C
13 and 14	?Cardamine hirsuta	Hairy Bitter-cress	W	C
14	?Sherardia arvensis (blue fl.)	Field Madder	W	C
	?Poa sp.	Meadow Grass	W	C
	Geranium molle	Dove's-foot Crane's-bill	W	C
	Sherardia arvensis (pink fl.)	Field Madder	W	C
	?	Grass	W	-
15	Plantago lanceolata	Ribwort Plantain	W	C
	Erodium cicutarium	Common Stork's-Bill	W	C
	Brassica rapa	Wild Turnip	N	C
	Ranunculus acris	Meadow Buttercup	W	C
	Stellaria media	Common Chickweed	W	C
16	Geranium lucidum	Shining Crane's-bill	W	L
	Myosotis scorpioides	Water Forget-me-not	W	C
	?Erysimum cheiranthoides	Treacle Mustard	W	C
	Onobrychis viciifolia	Sainfoin	W, N	L
	?Galium mollugo	Hedge Bedstraw	W	C
17	Capsella bursa-pastoris	Shepherd's-purse	W	C
	Sherardia arvensis	Field Madder	W	C
	Lamium amplexicaule	Henbit Dead-nettle	W	C
	Viola riviniana	Common Dog-violet	W	C
	Malus sylvestris	Crab Apple	W	C
18	Silene dioica	Red Campion	W	C
	Lamiastrum galeobdolon	Yellow Archangel	W	C
	Borago officinalis	Borage	N, G	L
	Silene alba	White Campion	W	C
	Silene vulgaris	Bladder Campion	W	C
19	Valeriana dioica	Marsh Valerian	W	L
	Sinapis arvensis	Charlock	W	C
	Potentilla erecta	Tormentil	W	C
	Hottonia palustris	Water-violet	W	L
	?Ranunculus trichophyllus	Thread-leaved Water-crowfoot	W	C
	Orchis mascula	Early-purple Orchid	W	C
	Fumaria officinalis	Common Fumitory	W	C
20	?Cerastium holosteoides	Common Mouse-ear	W	C
	Cymbalaria muralis	Ivy-leaved Toadflax	N	C
	Erophila verna	Common Whitlow-grass	W	C
21	?Tripleurospermum maritimum	Scentless Mayweed	W	C
	?Meum athamanticum	Spignel	W	L
	Prunus spinosa	Blackthorn	W	C
	?Geranium molle (white form)	Dove's-foot Crane's-bill	W	C
	Crataegus monogyna	Hawthorn	W	C
page 22	Rumex conglomeratus	Clustered Dock	W	C
	Vicia cracca	Tufted Vetch	W	C
	Bryonia dioica	White Bryony	W	C
23	Prunus avium	Wild Cherry	W	C
	Aesculus hippocastanum	Horse-chestnut	N, G	C
	Syringa vulgaris	Lilac	N, G	L
24	Capsella bursa-pastoris	Shepherd's-purse	W	C
	Valeriana dioica	Marsh Valerian	W	L
	Trifolium medium	Zigzag Clover	W	L
	Trifolium dubium	Lesser Trefoil	W	C
	Carex sp.	Sedge		
	Pinguicula vulgaris	Common Butterwort	W	C
	?Ranunculus acris	Meadow Buttercup	W	C
	Silene dioica	Red Campion	W	C
	Myosotis ?arvensis	Field Forget-me-not	W	C
	Trifolium medium	Zigzag Clover	W	L
	?Anthoxanthum odoratum	Sweet Vernal-grass	W	C
	Rumex acetosa	Common Sorrel	W	C
	Raphanus raphanistrum	Wild Radish	W	C
	Endymion non-scriptus	Bluebell	W	C
	Poterium sanguisorba	Salad Burnet	W	C
25	Equisetum telmateia	Great Horsetail	W	L
	Myosotis arvensis	Field Forget-me-not	W	C
	Arum maculatum	Lords-and-Ladies	W	C
	Chelidonium majus	Greater Celandine	W	C
	Barbarea vulgaris	Winter-cress	W	C
26	Centaurea scabiosa	Greater Knapweed	W	C
	Galium verum	Lady's Bedstraw	W	C
	Centaurea cyanus	Cornflower	W, G	R
	Fumaria officinalis	Common Fumitory	W	C
27	Narcissus pseudonarcissus	Wild Daffodil	W, G, N	L
	Potentilla anserina	Silverweed	W	C
	Pedicularis sylvatica	Lousewort	W	C
	Potentilla ?anglica	Trailing Tormentil	W	L
28	Chrysanthemum leucanthemum	Oxeye Daisy	W	C
	Galium odoratum	Woodruff	W	L
	Symphytum officinale	Common Comfrey	W	C
29	Laburnum anagyroides	Laburnum	G, N	L
	Geum urbanum	Wood Avens	W	C
	Ranunculus ficaria	Lesser Celandine	W	C
	Ranunculus arvensis	Corn Buttercup	W	L
	Ranunculus bulbosus	Bulbous Buttercup	W	C
30	Cheiranthus cheiri (2)	Wallflower	N, G	L
	Ranunculus aquatilis	Common Water-crowfoot	W	C
	Acinos arvensis	Basil Thyme	W	L
	Achillea millefolium	Yarrow	W	C
	Lotus corniculatus	Common Bird's-foot-trefoil	W	C
31	Crataegus monogyna (2 garden forms)	Hawthorn	G	
	Rubus caesius	Dewberry	W	C
	Rubus fruticosus	Bramble	W	C
32	Rhinanthus minor	Yellow Rattle	W	C
	Fragaria vesca	Wild Strawberry	W	C
	?Dactylorhiza incarnata	Early Marsh-orchid	W	L
	Vicia sepium	Bush Vetch	W	C
	Lotus uliginosus	Greater Bird's-foot-trefoil	W	C

	Scientific name	English name	Status	Common
page 33	Cardamine amara	Large Bitter-cress	W	L
	Lysimachia nemorum	Yellow Pimpernel	W	C
	?Lepidium latifolium	Dittander	W	L
	Sherardia arvensis	Field Madder	W	C
	Veronica beccabunga	Brooklime	W	C
34	Rumex acetosella	Sheep's Sorrel	W	C
	Stellaria holostea	Greater Stitchwort	W	C
	Viola arvensis	Field Pansy	W	C
	?Dactylis glomerata	Cock's-foot	W	C
	Geranium molle	Dove's-foot Crane's-bill	W	C
	Saxifraga spathularis x umbrosa	London Pride	G, N	L
	Sherardia arvensis	Field Madder	W	C
	Erodium cicutarium	Common Stork's-bill	W	C
	?Arabidopsis thaliana	Thale Cress	W	C
	Veronica chamaedrys	Germander Speedwell	W	C
35	Pinguicula vulgaris	Common Butterwort	W	C
	Rorippa nasturtium-aquaticum	Water-cress	W	C
	Ranunculus aquatilis	Common Water-crowfoot	W	C
	Polygala vulgaris	Common Milkwort	W	C
36	Knautia arvensis	Field Scabious	W	C
	Malva sylvestris	Common Mallow	W	C
	Convolvulus arvensis	Field Bindweed	W	C
	Prunella vulgaris	Selfheal	W	C
37	Chrysanthemum segetum	Corn Marigold	W	L
	Aesculus ?carnea	Horse Chestnut	G	
	Lithospermum arvense	Field Gromwell	W	L
	Saxifraga granulata	Meadow Saxifrage	W	L
38	Linaria vulgaris	Common Toadflax	W	C
	Clematis vitalba (fruit and flower)	Traveller's-joy	W	C
	?Heracleum sphondylium	Hogweed	W	C
39	?Fagopyrum esculentum	Buckwheat	G, N	L
	Vicia hirsuta	Hairy Tare	W	C
	Trifolium micranthum	Slender Trefoil	W	C
	Trifolium incarnatum	Crimson Clover	N, G	R
	Trifolium repens	White Clover	W	C
	Trifolium pratense	Red Clover	W	C
40	Kerria japonica	-	G	-
	Conium maculatum	Hemlock	W	C
	Viburnum lantana	Wayfaring-tree	W	C
	?Alopecurus pratensis	Meadow Foxtail	W	C
41	Dactylorhiza fuchsii	Common Spotted-orchid	W	C
	Euphorbia amygdaloides	Wood Spurge	W	C
	Dianthus gratianopolitanus	Cheddar Pink	W	R
	with Anthocharis cardamines	Orange-tip Butterfly	W	C
42	Ilex aquifolium (two forms)	Holly	W	C
	Circaea lutetiana	Enchanter's-nightshade	W	C
	Galium verum	Lady's Bedstraw	W	C
	Thymus drucei	Wild Thyme	W	C
	Circaea lutetiana (again)	-	-	-
43	Onobrychis viciifolia	Sainfoin	W, N	L
	Lathyrus pratensis	Meadow Vetchling	W	C
	Geum rivale	Water Avens	W	C
	Poterium sanguisorba	Salad Burnet	W	C
	Stellaria graminea	Lesser Stitchwort	W	C
	Veronica montana	Wood Speedwell	W	C
page 44	Pinguicula vulgaris	Common Butterwort	W	C
	Briza media	Quaking-grass	W	C
	Iris versicolor	-	G, N	R
	Solanum dulcamara	Bittersweet	W	C
45	Lathyrus odoratus	Sweet Pea	G	-
	Iris pseudacorus	Yellow Iris	W	C
	Lathyrus odoratus (again)	-	-	-
46	Campanula trachelium	Nettle-leaved Bellflower	W	L
	Centaurium erythraea	Common Centaury	W	C
	Campanula rotundifolia	Harebell	W	C
47	Dactylorhiza ?incarnata	Early Marsh-orchid	W	L
	Echium vulgare	Viper's-bugloss	W	C
	Sarothamnus scoparius	Broom	W	C
48	Sarothamnus scoparius	Broom	W	C
	Anthyllis vulneraria	Kidney Vetch	W	C
49	Veronica ?officinalis	Heath Speedwell	W	C
	Vicia angustifolia	Narrow-leaved Vetch	W	C
	Prunella vulgaris	Selfheal	W	C
	Geranium dissectum	Cut-leaved Crane's-bill	W	C
	Listera ovata	Common Twayblade	W	L
	with Abraxas grossulariata	Magpie moth	W	C
	Acinos arvensis	Basil Thyme	W	L
	Vicia sepium	Bush Vetch	W	C
50	Geranium robertianum	Herb-Robert	W	C
	with Tyria jacobaeae	Cinnebar Moth	W	C
	?Holcus lanatus	Yorkshire-fog	W	C
	Linum catharticum	Fairy Flax	W	C
	?Poa pratensis	Smooth Meadow-grass	W	C
	Ophrys apifera	Bee Orchid	W	L
51	Galium ?verum	Lady's Bedstraw	W	C
	Knautia arvensis	Field Scabious	W	C
	Tripleurospermum maritimum	Scentless Mayweed	W	C
	Odontites verna	Red Bartsia	W	C
52	Lonicera periclymenum	Honeysuckle	W	C
	Rosa canina	Dog Rose	W	C
	Rubus fruticosus	Bramble	W	C
53	Senecio jacobaea	Common Ragwort	W	C
	Sedum acre	Biting Stonecrop	W	C
	Aristolochia clematitis	Birthwort	G, N	L
	Lapsana communis	Nipplewort	W	C
54	Melilotus ?altissima	Tall Melilot	W, N	C
	Epilobium hirsutum	Great Willowherb	W	C
	?Erysimum cheiranthoides	Treacle Mustard	W	C
	Agrimonia eupatoria	Agrimony	W	C
55	Myosoton aquaticum	Water Chickweed	W	C
	Plantago media	Hoary Plantain	W	C
	Eriophorum angustifolium	Common Cottongrass	W	C
	Vicia ?sativa	Common Vetch	W	C
56	Erica tetralix	Cross-leaved Heath	W	C
	Oenanthe ?aquatica	Fine-leaved Water-dropwort	W	L
	?Prunus laurocerasus	Cherry Laurel	G, N	L
	Ajuga reptans	Bugle	W	C
	Viola tricolor	Wild Pansy	W	C
	Myosotis scorpioides	Water Forget-me-not		C

	Scientific name	English name	Status	Common
page 57	Scutellaria galericulata	Skullcap	W	C
	Geranium pratense	Meadow Crane's-bill	W	C
	Filipendula vulgaris	Dropwort	W	L
	Melilotus ?altissima	Tall Melilot	W, N	C
	?Cerastium arvense (flowers wrong)	Field Mouse-ear	W	C
58	Calystegia sylvatica	Large Bindweed	N	C
	Butomus umbellatus	Flowering-rush	W	L
	Chrysanthemum segetum	Corn Marigold	W	L
59	Sinapis arvensis	Charlock	W	C
	Galeopsis tetrahit	Common Hemp-nettle	W	C
	Conopodium majus	Pignut	W	C
	Betonica officinalis	Betony	W	C
	Sison amomum	Stone Parsley	W	L
	Hypericum ?androsaemum	Tutsan	W	L
60	Geranium dissectum	Cut-leaved Crane's-bill	W	C
	Ranunculus bulbosus	Bulbous Buttercup	W	C
	Aquilegia vulgaris	Columbine	W	L
	Lychnis flos-cuculi	Ragged Robin	W	C
61	?Phalaris arundinacea	Reed Canary-grass	W	C
	Melica uniflora	Wood Melick	W	C
	Deschampsia cespitosa	Tufted Hair-grass	W	C
	Luzula pilosa	Hairy Wood-rush	W	C
	Juncus inflexus	Hard Rush	W	C
	Lolium perenne	Perennial Rye-grass	W	C
62	Cerastium holosteoides	Common Mouse-ear	W	C
	Senecio jacobaea	Common Ragwort	W	C
	Lythrum salicaria	Purple-loosestrife	W	C
	Galium odoratum	Woodruff	W	L
	Sedum ?reflexum	Reflexed Stonecrop	G, N	L
63	Medicago sativa	Lucerne	N	L
	Hippocrepis comosa	Horseshoe Vetch	W	L
	Achillea ptarmica	Sneezewort	W	C
	Erica ?tetralix	Cross-leaved Heath	W	C
	?Phalaris arundinacea	Reed Canary-grass	W	C
	?Chamaemelum nobile	Chamomile	W	L
	Myosotis ?arvensis	Field Forget-me-not	W	C
64	Briza media (2)	Quaking-grass	W	C
	Aira caryophyllea	Silver Hair-grass	W	C
	Ballota nigra	Black Horehound	W	C
	?Poa pratensis	Smooth Meadow-grass	W	C
	?Arrhenatherum elatius	False Oat-grass	W	C
65	Sisymbrium officinale	Hedge Mustard	W	C
	Rorippa ?sylvestris	Creeping Yellow-cress	W	C
	Centaurea nigra	Common Knapweed	W	C
	Ranunculus sceleratus	Celery-leaved Buttercup	W	C
	Barbarea vulgaris	Winter-cress	W	C
66	Arctium lappa	Greater Burdock	W	C
	Dipsacus fullonum	Teasel	W	C
	Silybum marianum	Milk Thistle	N	L
67	Origanum vulgare	Marjoram	W	C
	Cichorum intybus	Chicory	W	C
	Hypericum ?perforatum	Perforate St John's-wort	W	C
	Melampyrum pratense	Common Cow-wheat	W	C
	Sonchus arvensis	Perennial Sow-thistle	W	C
68	Cruciata laevipes	Crosswort	W	C
	Origanum vulgare	Marjoram	W	C
	Calluna vulgaris	Heather	W	C
	Galeopsis angustifolia	Red Hemp-nettle	W	L

	Scientific name	English name	Status	Common
page 69	Vinca major	Greater Periwinkle	G, N	L
	Lysimachia nemorum	Yellow Pimpernel	**W**	C
	Helianthemum chamaecistus	Common Rockrose	W	C
	Acinos arvensis	Basil Thyme	W	L
	Polygonum ?lapathifolium with Arctia caja	Pale Persicaria Garden Tiger-moth (caterpillar)	W	C
	Diplotaxis tenuifolia	Perennial Wall-rocket	W	L
70	Arum maculatum (flower and fruit (2))	Lords-and-Ladies	W	C
	Sparganium erectum	Branched Bur-reed	W	C
	Scrophularia auriculata	Water Figwort	W	C
71	Philadelphus coronarius	Mock Orange	G, N	L
	Solanum nigrum	Black Nightshade	W	C
	Polygonum hydropiper	Water-pepper	W	C
	Tamarix anglica	Tamarisk	G, N	L
72	Hypericum ?perforatum	Perforate St John's-wort	W	C
	Ononis repens	Common Restharrow	W	C
	Hypericum ?perforatum (again)			
73	Veronica chamaedrys	Germander Speedwell	W	C
	Hypericum hirsutum	Hairy St John's-wort	W	L
	Ranunculus repens	Creeping Buttercup	W	C
	Foeniculum vulgare	Fennel	W, N	L
	Potentilla ?erecta	Tormentil	W	C
	Geranium molle	Dove's-foot Crane's-bill	W	C
74	Moehringia trinervia	Three-nerved Sandwort	W	C
	Anagallis arvensis	Scarlet Pimpernel	W	C
	Raphanus raphanistrum	Wild Radish	W	C
	Agrostemma githago	Corncockle	N	R
	Scutellaria galericulata	Skullcap	W	C
75	Jasminum ?officinale	Common Jasmine	G	
	Ligustrum vulgare	Wild Privet	W	C
	Achillea millefolium	Yarrow	W	C
	?Alopecurus myosuroides	Black-grass	W	C
	Achillea millefolium (again)			
	Sisymbrium officinale	Hedge Mustard	W	C
	Ulex minor	Dwarf Gorse	W	L
	Erica tetralix	Cross-leaved Heath	W	C
76	Epilobium montanum (white)	Broad-leaved Willowherb	W	C
	Epilobium montanum (pink)	Broad-leaved Willowherb	W	C
	Hypericum ?perforatum	Perforate St John's-wort	W	C
	Lysimachia nummularia	Creeping-Jenny	W	C
	Teucrium scorodonia	Wood Sage	W	C
	Circaea lutetiana	Enchanter's Nightshade	W	C
	Prunella vulgaris	Selfheal	W	C
77	Sarothamnus scoparius	Broom	W	C
	Euonymus europaeus	Spindle	W	C
	Cynoglossum officinale	Hound's-tongue	W	C
	Arbutus unedo	Strawberry-tree	G, W	R
	Jasminum ?officinale	Common Jasmine	G	
	Viburnum tinus	Laurustinus	G, N	R
78	Rosa rubiginosa	Sweet Briar	W	L
	Calluna vulgaris	Heather	W	C
	Swida sanguinea	Dogwood	W	C
	Symphoricarpos rivularis	Snowberry	G, N	L
	Berberis ?darwinii	Barberry	G	
	Cardamine hirsuta	Hairy Bitter-cress	W	C